Praises for the Book

"Few things are better than a good sit-down chat with a close girlfriend—especially when she knows what she's talking about. Author Drea Bauer becomes your newest close girlfriend and she knows what she's talking about. Like a combination of a relationship therapist and a character out of a Jane Austen novel, Bauer entertainingly delivers some pretty serious goods."

—Marianne Williamson, author of four #1 New York Times best sellers, including A Return to Love

"As an author, entrepreneur, and personal development coach, it's always refreshing when someone is able to give new insight into a popular topic. Drea Bauer has impressively found a way to combine unique strategies for online dating with cutting-edge techniques and psychology for personal development so that the reader not only learns how to date online, but also learns how to enhance the quality of their life!"

—Chris Salamone, New York Times and Wall Street Journal best-selling author

Awakened Dating

The Success Formula for Online Dating

Drea Bauer, JD

Charleston, South Carolina

Published in the United States of America by Pierucci Publishing.

This book is not meant for free distribution. For information about permission to reproduce selections from this book, write to Pierucci Publishing, PO Box 8067, Aspen, CO 81612.

ISBN 978-1-956257-01-4

Pierucci Publishing, PO Box 8067, Aspen, CO 81612

www.pieruccipublishing.com

Acknowledgments

In writing this book, I am overflowing with gratitude for all the lessons I have learned in this lifetime and for all those who have assisted me on my path. My family has been perfect for my self-growth and for loving all those less-than-perfect parts of me. My mother is devotional in her love and efforts to make her children successful. She has given all of herself so that I might experience more in my life than I ever dreamed possible. I am blessed with her unyielding love and encouragement.

My grandparents were instrumental in my mother's life, as well as my brother's and mine. They provided for us on a level that was well outside what they had ever received from their parents. It seems they were instinctively guided by deep, intrinsic love for all of us. Every selfless act they have done has made me who I am today. I am blessed beyond any words I can offer. To them both, now in Heaven, I love and cherish every moment spent in your divine company. The memories will take me through a lifetime until we are united.

My brother is an inspiration in my life. I spent so much of my youth trying to keep up. I spent so much of my adult life admiring his work for my state. He is constantly evolving and giving even more of himself to others. His dedication to his constituents and his family moves me. I am honored with his love and support no matter what road I choose, and in return I gift him with the same.

To my father, I love and appreciate all the contributions you offer the world. I am thankful to have your strength from which to learn and love.

To my extraordinary confidant Cindy, I miss you dearly. Your intellect, beauty, and wisdom never ceased to amaze me! I know you are now my angel in Heaven as you were on Earth.

To my sisters by choice, Emma and Noushin, thank you for giving me that constant feedback in order that I might improve who I am, and how I show up in the world. Thank you for your unwavering love, while pushing me to be the best version of myself.

To my readers, I am blessed to share all the amazing information I have acquired in this lifetime. Everything you do today predetermines your tomorrow. The current conditions in our lives are a direct reflection of the decisions we have made; it's simply the law of cause and effect. Your future is generated by the choices you are making in every second of your life. In choosing to read this book today, your growth will be evident in your life tomorrow. As it is said, you reap what you sow.

A portion of the proceeds from the sale of this book will be donated to the Claire's Place Foundation. Claire's Place Foundation, Inc. is a non-profit organization that benefits children and families affected by Cystic Fibrosis. Claire's Place Foundation is named in honor of my friend Claire Wineland, now another of my angels in Heaven. Claire lived those words so eloquently expressed by Mahatma Gandhi: "Be the change you wish to see in the world." I am so filled with admiration for her service while on Earth and am so very proud to have been her friend. For more information see http://clairesplacefoundation.org/.

"Each of us has a unique part to play in the healing of the world."

Marianne Williamson

Table of Contents

Disclaimer

No part of this book is authorized for reproduction or transmission in any form, including but not limited to printing or photocopying, electronic or recorded, without written permission from the author.

The author makes no representations or warranties as to the accuracy or completeness of this book. The author hereby disclaims any and all warranties or guarantees, express or implied, in relation to this book or any promotional materials involving said work. The author shall not be liable for any physical, psychological, commercial, financial, or other damages, including, but not limited to, incidental, consequential, or special. The contents of this book are designed only for informational and motivational purposes. The contents are simply the personal expression and opinions of the author and are not intended to be relied upon as expert advice, nor medical advice, nor any endorsement of any personal development program(s). The author is not rendering any legal, psychological, medical, professional advice or other services.

The author is not responsible for any specific mental or physical health needs that may require medical supervision. This book should not be used to diagnose or treat any physiological or psychological medical conditions. For diagnosis or treatment of any ailment, consult your own physician. The author is not liable for any damages or negative repercussions from any treatment, action, application or preparation, or lack thereof to any person reading or following the information contained in this book. The author

Chapter One:

Access Your Inner Beauty Online

Online dating, which includes both websites and phone apps, can open a world of new dating experience. It can be made fun and easy; let me save you the years of trial and error in figuring out the best methods for success. The right skill set will make your online dating a breeze, and actually enjoyable. Think about it, in reality you can save time. You can pre-date right in the comfort of your own home in your pj's. No going out with a guy only to find his religion or political views are intolerable to you. No accidental flirting with the guy at the bar who's married or taken. No spending an evening with a blind date with whom you share no common interest. And, even better, no driving, no dressing, and no prepping. I have learned the tricks of the trade and I'm going to share them all with you. So come with me and enjoy the process of finding your exceptional man while developing your inner goddess through online dating. I'm so excited for you I can hardly stand it.

This book is an instruction manual not only on how to date online, but more importantly, how to become an exceptional you. Without exception, you are exceptional. Sometimes we just need to find the best resources to access that inner beauty. This book is chock-full with all the knowledge I've been compiling my entire life. No category of life is left untouched. It covers psychology, physical appearance, body language, emotions, and energy—all the success strategies I've studied and applied to make my own life everything I could ever dream. It fully explains how I used the Internet to access my inner beauty. You can use these exact success strategies in your own life to make it EVERYTHING you desire. The Internet is a remarkable learning tool in cognitive psychology and human behavior. Through your interactions online, you can learn what guides your actions and the actions of others. By tapping into this knowledge, you can better develop yourself and your dating skills.

I'm a lawyer. I know how to analyze, but I had to get back to the basics: How to trust my intuition, How to be a woman, How to be full from the inside out, How to not be dependent on anything external to bring me true happiness, How to date successfully for pleasure and personal growth, How to become the woman who would attract the quality of people I desired into my life. I now find delight in the dating process and discover more about myself through every encounter. I have surrendered to the learning process. My personal journey has permitted me to find fulfillment in every interaction. I am completely present and enjoy each occasion in the company of a date, friends, family, or just myself. The more I appreciate myself, the more others appreciate me.

You, too, can cultivate all the beauty within yourself to reach your full potential. Not only will you master the online dating scene, you will master yourself. This book will impart inspiration and techniques for you to access your inner goddess by experimenting with online dating. Pay special attention to the *Crown Jewels*. These will offer gems of information to utilize in your online dating experience and life in general. If you do the internal work, you will witness your own personal transformation. You will be so overflowing with radiance that others will gravitate into your company. More importantly than finding a partner, you will find yourself through this online endeavor. You will even want to hang out more with *you.*

Throughout this book, I will use what I label my Groundhog Day approach. What this means is that you try a tactic on a man, and if it doesn't work, alter your approach for the next man, and if that doesn't work, try a new approach...and so on until you find the one that does. You can use this to revise your online profile as well. This Groundhog Day strategy is cross-contextual, meaning it works in all areas of life. If you aren't getting what you want at work, in your relationships with your friends or family, or even in your spiritual connection, try another approach. And if you're still not getting what you want, try something different, and if that still doesn't work, change your approach again. "If you do what you've always done, you'll get what you always got." (Mark Twain)

Crown Jewel: My Groundhog Day approach means you test a strategy on an issue, and if it doesn't work, try a different approach. And if that doesn't work, try another approach, and so on, until you find the one that does work.

You have all the resources you need within you. You just need to get creative with those resources. Throughout this book you are going to learn how to tap into all those internal resources buried within your subconscious self. You will discover your ability to utilize all that ever-present knowledge you harbor deep below your conscious mind. You will begin to identify the signals your infinite wisdom provides through your intuitive responses. Once you are able to access your inner guidance, you will find there are no unresourceful people, only unresourceful states, which is a common idea among practitioners of personal development. If you find yourself in a lull, jump out of it. Literally change your physical state, and it will change your emotional state. It's cause and effect. Keep changing your state until you find an energy you want to work with.

Online dating has allowed me to refine my skills of conversation and connection. These skills are invaluable in interactions with both men and women in my life. I have recognized that for me, the purpose of life is connection to others. It's no longer about what I'm buying at the store, it's about the interaction with the clerk. Not one of us is truly independent. The gift is our interdependence on one another for survival. Isn't it true that we will do more for others than ourselves? Think about a friend who has a project. Aren't you always looking for people you can connect your friend with who will be of assistance? Are you as eager to ask for help on your own project? Oftentimes we will go outside our comfort zone to help others while we won't push as hard to promote ourselves. We accomplish much more with a collective energy than would ever be possible alone. Our knowledge as a society builds so quickly—it's how technology has jumped by leaps and bounds. We don't reinvent the wheel each time; we build on what those before us have discovered.

In dating and in all areas of life, these interpersonal skills you are developing will be essential to your evolution. Most people set their goals so low that they never attain anything that really matters to them. They play it safe in life—making it safely to death. They will do more to keep what they have than to get what they really want. You have the ability to create your future. Your soul expansion will determine which path to your destiny you choose. The higher you vibrate, the higher your reciprocal energy will vibrate. The people and opportunities that surround you will be more of an equivalent to those you seek. The more conscious you become, the more you will comprehend how much you don't know. The more you appreciate how much you don't know, the more you will be in flow. Aw, what a beautiful feat—when you get out of your own way. When you get out of your head and into your heart.

Crown Jewel: "Whether you think you can, or you think you can't—you're right." (Henry Ford)

I've now dedicated my life to learning and growing as a person. I have been searching for and preparing myself for my exceptional man. Online dating has afforded me the opportunity to cultivate my dating skills and my person as a whole. I have grown into the woman I have always desired to be. I have learned to be both feminine and gracious, to be giving of myself while allowing men to give to me as well. I now practice wholehearted presence in dating and in all of my life. In every moment, no matter what I am doing or whom I am with, I am fully engaged in the experience. I used to live my life either looking back at the past in regret or looking forward to the future in anticipation. Now I am fully invested in each tiny speck of time and value the experience for whatever it may offer. I am full internally, so when I am with others, I am not seeking to be filled up, but to share the moment. No matter whose company I keep, I'm a better woman for my experience of online dating—and you can be, too.

Crown Jewel: Practice presence in every moment. No matter what you are experiencing, you will either enjoy more, learn more, or give more, whatever need be.

Yes, I'm a romantic. I'm looking for my soul mate—that perfect fit for me. I want a partner who is compatible with me for the long haul, but more than merely finding a mate, I want to be the happy person I was born to be and savor every minute of life. I believe life is meant to be enjoyed. We spend most of our time in the process of working toward our goals. Once we reach our goal, there's always a little thrill, and then a new goal. I'm going to find pleasure in the process and celebrate my wins every day. Practicing presence in every moment is the art of fully experiencing whatever activity you are engaging in. I wish the same for all of you; to really find the pleasure in the journey towards your goals. I don't believe in scarcity. My outlook on life postulates that our resources are plentiful, and I have immense gratitude for all the abundance surrounding me. I am certain there are enough happiness and enough prosperity to go around. That means there are enough exceptional men for all of you exceptional women.

I'm an overachiever, and I'm going to work every tool I can find to improve myself and get all I want out of life. Isn't it true an increasing majority of our time is spent communicating online? Whether it is for work or play, all forms of communication are gravitating to the Internet and phone applications (apps). Throughout this book reference will be made to "online" which will also include apps. New social and business websites and apps are popping up daily, each with its specific niche, like Facebook, Instagram, LinkedIn, Skype, and Zoom. Whether it is for business or pleasure, for conferences or chatting, everyone is connecting online. The human need for connectedness has led to the creation of these websites, apps, and tools, which are the modern evolutions of human communication. This communication meets our needs for social and interpersonal interaction, virtually.

In today's world, if you are looking for a partner, you can't deny online dating is an amazing resource. The Internet superhighway has turned our world into a neighborhood; it's an "online community." As years pass the dating pool gets smaller, if only because more people get married. Online, there are more fish in the pond. You can cast your Internet to scoop up your exceptional man. It opens such vast opportunities never before available in history. Not so many years ago, people were limited by social class, ethnicity, or religion. How blessed are we to be free to engage in relationships with whomever we choose. Now you aren't limited by anything—not even proximity. You are a brilliant woman, and this book will fast forward you to all the benefits online dating can impart to you. You are going to capitalize on all my trials and errors, which have been the greatest teachers in my life.

Crown Jewel: More men are online dating than women. The odds are already stacked in your favor.

Chapter Two:

A Little about the Author

As a child, I spent every summer down at the beach in Charleston with my grandparents. They were the best Granny and Papa a girl could wish for. Their full expression of deep love and devotion to one another is inspirational. Papa and Granny were together forever. I aspire to have such a wonderful, loving relationship that stands the test of time— and lasts an eternity. I loved my time at the beach building sand castles; playing in the ocean; boogie boarding on the waves; investigating Fort Moultrie, an old battleground from the Revolutionary and Civil Wars; and exploring Charles Towne Landing, a historic park that makes you feel as if you were one of the original settlers of Charleston—all very fond memories of my youth.

Papa would drive my brother and me around to his jobs as a "master builder" in his work van. He was an extraordinary artist working with wood. He handcrafted everything from custom houses to church organs. In his van he built a special seat for me to sit on, just the right size, and a wall full of cabinets to house his tools and snacks, including Vienna sausage and other nonperishables. Papa used to build every toy I wanted out of wood. I once wanted a baby stroller for my dolls. So, guess what? I got one. It wasn't your traditional cheap plastic baby carriage, but a handcrafted wooden carriage for my dolls to ride in style. One time my brother wanted some toy guns. Well, you guessed it—you couldn't break those wooden guns, and we had enough for all the kids in the neighborhood. The battle was on. You know how most girls had the plastic kitchen set with a table and chairs, a refrigerator, a stove and oven? Not mine. Those wooden toys stood the test of time. They're still at mom's house to this day.

Now, Granny managed the home and that was no easy task. She was the top chef and the interior decorator. Every season saw a changing of the decoration guard. Every room of the house was festive with garb of fall or spring, Christmas or Easter, St. Patrick's Day or Valentine's Day—whatever holiday was around the corner. Everything was decorated, from lampshades to doorknobs; she would have garlands or some form of ornamental embellishments covering every nook and cranny of the house. She also had non-seasonal collections of delightful trinkets. I now house the cow collection, moo. Granny was a phenomenal cook. She would whip up the best homemade pizza with all the extras, banana nut bread, and biscuits...mmm biscuits. I loved to eat the dough raw. I know, I know, but I didn't know then. What doesn't kill you... It was first class all the way with Papa and Granny.

I had a real passion for dancing and singing throughout my childhood. My girlfriends and I would take turns dancing to the radio. Barbie would even get in on the action. I loved Barbies. I had the best time dressing them up and prancing them around. She never had to think about finding a partner; she only had one option back then, Ken. I took tap dance lessons for years and a few voice lessons here and there. I loved to sing every chance I got, but mainly when no one was around. I never really thought I was good enough for an audience. And, now I actually sing professionally with a Gullah Gospel Choir, The Plantation Singers. I am honored to have been welcomed into their group, and into their community. They are my extended family.

I had always put it out there that I wanted to go to law school, although I really never thought I was smart enough. Even as early as grammar school, I would dress up in a suit on career day with a badge that read, "Drea Bauer, Esquire." As I neared the end of undergrad at USC, I took all the preparatory steps to apply to law school. I was still thinking I wasn't really bright enough to get a high enough score on the admissions test (LSAT) to get me in. But mom was certain; she enrolled me in an LSAT prep course. Then the day of the test came. As I started the exam, I got cold sweats. I almost walked out.

On the LSAT, if you take the exam more than once, they don't take the highest score, they average them. One bad exam and your chances of getting into any law school are done. Guess what? All my powers of manifestation worked. I did the work and put it out to the universe, and there you go. I got into the only school I applied to, USC.

My first year of law school, I really struggled. I knew the law, but I didn't understand the process of applying it to the cases. I was fortunate enough to land a summer clerkship with a firm in Charleston. I bought the best law school test prep book I could find. After working during the days, I dedicated the rest of my free time to really study the testing process and learn the skills to ace the exam. I spent countless hours reading, studying, and taking practice tests. That was the key. The next two years were a breeze. Don't get me wrong—I studied hard, but I knew how to take the test and do remarkably well because I had learned the skill set from the book.

Crown Jewel: You can learn any skill you choose if you do your homework. Research the best resources, study the technique of others who have gone before you, immerse yourself in the learning, and practice, practice, practice.

Right out of law school, I got a job as a judicial law clerk. My judge was an amazing man, and I loved the job, but clerkships are only one year long. After completing the judicial clerkship, I was hired as a staff attorney with a real estate law firm. I worked for a branch of that statewide firm in Charleston. The man who was running the firm went into private practice a few years after I started, and what do you know? Who took over? I was a bit intimidated at the daunting opportunity before me, but knew I couldn't pass it up. I was the managing attorney for that law firm for many years and was successful at it. I'm great at putting systems in place and following up. I'm a hard worker and don't mind putting forth the work to achieve the ultimate results.

During my educational years, I didn't have mature relationships with men. I guess that's not so uncommon. I had a high school sweetheart but never a serious relationship until my last year of college. That was my first real "boyfriend." I dated him for many years, and we got engaged. The diamond ring was gorgeous, and bigger than I could have imagined. I even bought the dress, but somehow my heart couldn't let me do it. Then a series of exclusive relationships ensued, all attempts to find my true soulmate. Each ended when my delusion of my prince ended. I attempted to apply the same skill set to dating that had brought me success in school and work. I looked for every book out there.

I studied diligently, but still nothing. Then, five years ago, I started what I call my spiral upward. The first thing I did was listen to Joel Osteen's *Get Your Best Life Now* CDs, then I went to a Tony Robbins conference. I had never attended any type of motivational or self-development conference in my life. The last day of the conference, he sold me. I bought the entire Master University Program, which is three live conferences, each lasting several days. Then I came home and listened to Joel again, and you know what? Joel and Tony say the same things. All the great teachers do. It's the delivery that's different. It's just like all the best athletes have coaches who use the same visualization techniques that self-development speakers share. They all coach you to visualize winning the race or achieving the goal. It's simply different methods of teaching geared to different areas of life.

Crown Jewel: If you have a goal, visualize yourself attaining it. Make certain you feel the emotion of having successfully accomplished the goal. You can't simply think your way to your goal; you must do the work and capture the positive emotion of successfully attaining the goal so you vibrate at the level that will attract your goal.

Now that I had this new set of tools, I had to unlearn a bunch of misinformation. As young women, we were taught never to rely on a man. That translates into do it yourself, take care of yourself, don't do for him because he won't do for you. That translates into be a man. I now lovingly embrace the polarity of men and women. What a sacred gift our creator has bestowed on us: what one gender excels in complements the other and vice versa. My personal growth has led me to a new way of thinking—a beautiful new way of seeing the world. I cherish this new outlook on men, the world, and my life.

In my personal growth, I have graduated from Tony Robbins' Master University and Leadership programs; become a Neuro Linguistic Programming (NLP) practitioner; completed extensive hours training personally with David Deida (author of *Way of the Superior Man*); been inducted as a Oneness Blessing Giver; attended PAX training with Allison Armstrong; sat in silence for eleven hours a day at a ten-day Vipassana Meditation Retreat; been certified in Temporal

Dynamics and Hypnotherapy; joined the sisterhood of Mama Gina; and, studied meditation with Joe Dispenza. I am excited by new growth opportunities, and love to explore and learn more about the issues I feel are most important to my evolution.

Since beginning my spiral upward, I have disciplined my exercise habits, cleaned up my eating habits, become a yogi, performed aerial acrobats, enhanced my peer group (tons of amazing new friends all over the world), quit my desk job, paid off all my debt, walked a red carpet at a major movie premiere, had a speaking line on a soap opera, continuously had a positive outlook, developed better style, become a Deeksha Blessing Giver, officiated numerous weddings, completed a ten-day meditation retreat, executive produced an environmentally conscious animation, attended the Sundance Film Festival, won the Bel-Air Film Festival, regularly performed professionally singing and dancing, and, have extensively traveled the states and abroad—just to name my favorites. A big success was the fact that I totally changed my drinking patterns so that I have a completely healthy relationship with alcohol. Now I rarely drink; however, on occasion you might find me enjoying a great glass of Bordeaux. I implement the strategies I've learned all over the planet in my own life and share them with others. I have learned so much about myself and this astounding world in which we live. Every culture is so unique with its own style and energy. I recently started a new bucket list and realized how many things I had already experienced that would complete my lifetime list. What a revelation.

One of the biggest discoveries I had during my self-development journey is that I'm inherently, extremely feminine. Would you believe that even though I so loved to dance as a child, for many years I quit dancing altogether until one day at a Tony Robbins seminar? Tony instructed everyone to close their eyes, then encouraged the women to move in any way they felt. I was embarrassed for people to even catch a glimpse of me attempting to dance. I felt I wasn't good enough to be seen in public, but this was a safe environment where the women were encouraged to express themselves through their bodies. Before that seminar, I had developed such a shell that I wouldn't even permit my own femininity to be released. I had a breakthrough; I had been using all the masculine traits that successfully propelled me in the scholastic and professional environments in the rest of my life as well. My core has always been feminine, but I was wearing a masculine armor and was so attached to it that I didn't know how to bring down the shield.

Nowadays, you can't get me off the dance floor. I'll shake it like a Polaroid picture all night long. I love to move every inch of my being—from my head to my toes and everything in between. It makes me feel so alive and vibrant. I take classes every chance I get—belly dancing, salsa, shag, hip-hop. I love them all, but my favorite is free-form, encompassing any movement I choose. I love to close my eyes and move every part of my body to the rhythm coursing through my veins. It allows me to express my loving effervescence and opens my heart. In my opinion, dance is one of those things you can't mess up. I don't care how tone deaf you are or how much rhythm you lack. It's like prayer: no matter how you do it, it can't be wrong.

Crown Jewel: Dancing is like prayer: no matter who you are or how you do it, you can't get it wrong. Energetically—prayer, meditation, and dancing are all more powerful when done in groups.

Every year I'm getting better and better. Mentally, I'm never distraught or down anymore. The words simply aren't part of my language patterns any longer. Every now and again, I find myself in a perplexing or challenging situation. I use all the skills I have learned the past five years to quickly resolve the challenge and my animosity toward the experience. Physically, I am in the best shape of my life. Even though I loved to dance as a child, I never did anything else athletic. Now I'm a pretty darn good yogi, doing everything from downward dog to headstands, with a few splits in between. I have recently taken up the aerial silks, which is like those performed in Cirque du Soleil. A long, silk piece of material hangs from the ceiling, and I climb it and perform acrobatic stunts, all without a net. I'm even scared of heights, but I'm doing it. The fact that I am able to perform aerial silks probably amazes *me* more than anyone I share it with. Spiritually, well, at this point of my life, everything is spiritually connected. It affects every move I make, every thought I think—it is me.

Chapter Three:

Online Dating Is an Optimal Way to Meet Men

I began to date online because I felt I had completely worked over the restaurant/bar scene. It was as if I knew every man in town, but maybe I just knew everyone who frequented the same places I did. I was out of school and self-employed, which limited my interaction with potential candidates. I decided I was going to test other options for introductions to dating prospects. I did tons of research on where to meet eligible men and explored them all. I went to grocery stores, restaurants, sporting events, conferences, coffee shops, hardware stores, church, and one person even suggested the library—shhh. I'm not saying these aren't great places to meet men; I still suggest you use them all. You never want to get so addicted to cyberspace that you stop engaging in real life. In my pursuit of love, I even sent handwritten thank you notes, as one book instructed, to people who had set me up on blind dates. I kept pounding the pavement, but I wasn't really even going on many dates to practice the new courtship techniques I had been studying.

I wanted the opportunity to go out with more men, but I wasn't about to be so desperate as to go online to find a date. I had an image in my community and with my friends; I wasn't going to stoop to that level. It was a small town and everyone would know. I'd be totally ashamed—but wait a minute, wouldn't they only know if they, too, were dating online? I pondered the question. Still, I thought, there is a stigma attached to people who online date. I wasn't going to risk people finding out. I was in a quandary. I knew there were countless gentlemen to date online, and I wanted so much to find some new exceptional men to go out with, yet I was scared by the imaginary peer pressure I had self-imposed. I just knew marvelous men were right there waiting for me. All I had to do was join an online dating service, and there would be dozens, if not hundreds, of quality men.

Crown Jewel: There are hundreds of dating sites, each with thousands, and up to millions, of members.

The day I wrote my profile, I had decided I would use a big city, Atlanta, Georgia to place my profile since I lived in a smaller town in South Carolina. I was still embarrassed that I, a well-known, attractive, successful attorney couldn't find an exceptional partner. After several hours of tweaking out an exceptional profile, I found myself proud and almost boastful of who I was online and the profile I had created. In reality, if we really knew how little (time) people actually thought about us, we'd be insulted. You know what? I posted that profile right where I lived in Charleston, South Carolina. My profile was clever, insightful, and funny. It explicitly showed who I was and what I was about. Though I was certainly not a model, the pictures were lovely and captured my true essence. In the process of creating my profile, I had become comfortable with who I was in that profile and the fact that there was certainly nothing shameful about looking for a quality man. I was a resourceful woman using every outlet available to locate my exceptional man. You know what else? All that "peer pressure" I had worried about never even existed. It was a story I had created about how "I thought" people would react. It was what "I thought" people would think.

That was several years ago, and now online dating has become mainstream. In today's world everyone is networking online. Marketing research shows that nearly 40% of new relationships begin online. Everybody is using cyberspace to connect, even if they aren't saying it. When was the last time a friend told you he or she met a date "through a mutual friend"? We all know who that friend is. I chose what I believed to be the longest running and largest dating websites. With advanced technology, the site was user friendly and offered overwhelming numbers of men. I did my homework. I wanted the best odds of finding an exceptional man. I'm a big believer in the 80/20 rule, and I was going to make certain I opted for the best site to get the best results.

The 80/20 rule, also known as the Pareto Principle, means 20 percent of your effort gives you 80 percent of your return. This means 80 percent of output comes from 20 percent of input. The rule comes from the Italian economist Vilfredo Pareto, who in 1906 determined that 80 percent of Italy's wealth was controlled by 20 percent of the population. It is a well-accepted rule in sales and marketing and is cross-contextual, again meaning it applies everywhere in life. Therefore, you should focus primarily on those tasks that provide the most results. Think about it: isn't it better to concentrate your efforts on those activities that return the most benefit with the least effort? It's the cost-benefit analysis. Is the energy you have to expend worth the return on investment you are going to receive?

Crown Jewel: Remember that 20 percent of your effort gives you 80 percent of your return. Pick those tasks that are effective at getting the job done, and then perform those tasks in an efficient manner.

I always applied this rule in school without knowing it existed. In those classes in which I knew it would take a substantial amount of extra time to get that A, I opted to do an insignificant amount of work in comparison and take the B. You are probably aware that our planet's resources are disproportionately dispersed, with 20 percent of the population controlling about 80 percent of the money and materials. Similarly, in sales, it is commonly known that 20 percent of your customers give you 80 percent of your sales. Rather than spend hours attending events in which I had no interest or going on blind dates when I knew nothing of the suitor in advance, I decided to get resourceful and figure out a way to find dates with qualities more in line with my ideal mate. Using the 80/20 rule, you can cut out all time dabbling in activities that don't get you much closer to your goal and find your exceptional self and your exceptional man in less time, conserving your energy for better use.

When choosing a dating site, research how long they have been in business and how many current subscribers they have. Many sites show members as active who haven't been on the site in years. Categorically, free sites want to keep the profiles up to appear to have more users. You want to determine what search technology they provide. Some sites allow you to search based on physical attributes, some on common interests, and some even on specific word searches. Many have automated services to directly send you prospects matching the characteristics you specify. Other sites do the all matching for you and don't allow you to search any profiles. Evaluate to determine if the tools on the site are user-friendly and self-explanatory.

Many sites charge a monthly fee that's only around the price of a movie for two. The longer the commitment you sign up for, of course, the lower the cost per month. There are completely free dating sites available; however, sometimes services are limited for free members. Most paid dating sites implement automated account renewals.

This means that before your subscription expires, a payment to your credit card on file will automatically be processed, and access to your account will remain unaffected. You want to make yourself familiar with the rules of the site, as well as the rules of the game.

Crown Jewel: A wink, a nudge, a poke, or a swipe is an option on sites to express interest in another user. Throughout this book I will refer to these as an "indication of interest." It is an overt flirt, virtually.

Your user information and profile do NOT show up in Google or other search engines on any of the dating sites I have researched. Many dating sites offer a free trial run. Those sites may require a temporary profile to login; others permit any and all non-subscribers to peruse profiles at any time. This means on some sites, individuals who are neither paid members nor trial users are able to randomly search profiles but may not interact with members. Unless hidden, your profile may be visible to anyone searching the site. Be careful not to reveal any personal information you would not want others to have access to. Your address and the name you provide under account information are not public information; nor do paid members have any way to access your personal account settings. You are a smart, exceptional woman; keep your safety goggles on when googling at men online and enjoy it. Online dating can be totally safe and totally fun.

Crown Jewel: Create a separate email account just for online dating so your other personal or business emails won't be mixed up with your dating life. You don't want to overload your inbox. Some sites systematically send you automated emails for any communication to you from other users. Some sites do not have a disable option for this service.

I know it's true that many people still think of online dating as taboo, but isn't it also true that some people think dating people from the work place is taboo? Others think meeting someone in a bar or a club is taboo. Is it really a better story to tell about having met your husband "at a bar"? Doesn't that imply impaired judgment? Some people complain that online dating is a scam because people lie, and others think it's not safe—but if you apply all the skills I'll explain in this book, you'll know how to protect yourself and make the most of your online dating opportunities. Isn't it true that people lie, no matter where you find them? You always have to use your intuition, whether you meet a guy in a restaurant or online. Isn't it also true there are liars at school, at work, and worse yet, at church? We are constantly allowing our gut to guide us in everyday interactions, and you will use those same feelings to guide you in this process, along with a few other tips to make certain you never put yourself at risk. Online dating can be safer and less imposing than the offline dating scene when you learn those skills.

People who are intimidated by the bar scene, feel shy or have "no game" are able to become an extrovert online. The individual with "no game" may appear to have it all "on paper" but be unsuccessful in interactions with members of the opposite sex. These types may find themselves nervous and acting inappropriately for no apparent reason. Online pre-dating provides a safe and comfortable means to build rapport. If you're shy in person, it's a great resource to expand your market. You don't have to approach or be approached randomly, making "small talk" to determine if you have any common interests. Even people with great communication skills often get tired of the bar or club scene. I have read this exact statement in countless profiles. You can utilize my Groundhog Day approach to refine your pre-dating skills before you move on to perfect your offline dating skills. You can test out different strategies when engaging men online until you find what works for you. Now that you're prepared to join the online scene, let's do the important work and get your energy and attitude up for the task at hand.

Chapter Four:

The Goddess of Goodness You Were Born to Be

Nobody likes a Negative Nancy—and that's not who you truly are at your core. You're an exceptional woman prepared to find her exceptional man. Men love happy, feminine women. Do the work and know your true self, your individual gifts, your love, and your depth. Then share them. Don't save them for a rainy day. Burn the candles, dry your hands on decorative hand towels, and wear your Sunday "best" clothes. Today and every day is a special occasion. Use your talents every chance you get. The more you use your talents, the more talents you are bestowed. Online dating is the perfect exercise to cultivate those exceptional qualities within you that will attract your exceptional man. You get to practice pulling out your internal goddess.

Let the world see the goddess of goodness you were put on earth to be. Wear your smile proudly to show all the love you have inside. Smiles are contagious and make everyone happy. Men always love to see a woman smile; if you are happy, they're doing their job. You can work a smile from the inside out or from the outside in. If you are happy, you naturally smile. If you smile, even if you are not authentically happy, you can't help but feel better. The proof is in the pudding—try it. It will elevate your mood and bring on a more upbeat overall disposition. Once your energy is higher, you will attract people and things resonating with that higher vibrational level. If you're having a tough day, it's all the more reason to put on a smile. If you grin and bear it, it will make it bearable.

Crown Jewel: You can work emotions from the inside out or from the outside in. Try it with a smile. Try it with confidence. Try it with any quality you want to flourish. Fake it till you make it.

If you find yourself feeling down, find the tools that pick you up. Make a list of all the activities you love to engage in that raise your spirits and make you cheerful. The list below will stimulate your thought process so that you might create your own Happy Times List. Pick activities you could do on a moment's notice to uplift your energy instantaneously. Include some activities that don't require any money, planning, or other people to engage in. It could be watching a sitcom or a funny movie. Maybe it's petting your kitty cat or walking your dog, or maybe it's going through family photos. If you don't know what makes you happy, how can you expect your partner to? Create your own list of specific activities that energize you and make you joyful. Have more ways to be happy than sad. I know your ultimate goal is to be ecstatic. Your "happily ever after" is based on your being happy, not on your finding a man who can "make you happy." First you must access your own internal happiness and allow that to fill you up. Allow yourself to be open; allow your love to flow, expecting nothing in return.

Happy Times List: viewing TV shows, watching movies, listening to music, dancing, singing, loving on pets, visiting the zoo, hiking, exercising, reading positive books, listening to positive audio, visiting new fun places, learning new things, skipping, smiling, laughing, praising yourself out loud, communicating with friends or family, organizing stuff, decorating, recollecting gratitude, walking on the beach, doing something for someone else, meditating, participating in a prayer/blessing group, praying in solitude, detoxing in a sauna, practicing yoga, going through photos, relaxing in a massage, deep breathing, journaling, soaking in a bubble bath, meditating in nature, swimming in the ocean, eating yummy foods, and making a list of funny memories or jokes.

As a woman, tap into your feminine essence with any of the following: dance in any way you feel; breathe into every part of your being; shake every part of your body; look into a mirror and sing "You Are So Beautiful"; tell yourself "I love you" and mean it; sing in the car or at a karaoke bar; play with your pets; love on your children; eat sweets; watch a good romantic film; or read a good romance novel. All these open your heart to the love that you are. Men love to witness women in their femininity—it's what makes you different from him; it's what makes him cherish you. You are a unique goddess; embrace your differences. Every experience you have ever had, every piece of you makes the spectacular being that you are. Appreciate all those parts of you. Every move you have ever made, everything that is within you has gotten you to this moment right now when you are ready for your exceptional man to show up. When you open your heart, you radiate your core feminine energy. It is your sacred gift to the world; unveil it. Your exceptional man will not be able to resist your glow. He will witness your free-flowing femininity before you utter a word. Give your attention to your internal goddess and she will grow, and he will gravitate to her.

Feminine Times List: dance; sing; breathe; kiss; love on animals; get a massage, facial, manicure, or pedicure; do a photo shoot; shop; enjoy a mud bath, sauna, hot tub, shower, or bubble bath; put on makeup; get a makeover; wear pink panties, dresses, heels, lipstick, or hair bows; eat sweets, or chocolate; flirt; smell flowers; read or watch a love story.

What you focus your attention on is what gets bigger. Think about it: if you constantly look for the pink elephant in the room, that's all you see; but if you focus on the eyes of your true love, you are oblivious to anything else in the room. Look in the mirror. What do you see? Don't focus on the areas you don't like. Literally bring your eyes to focus only on the areas you do like. If you don't like your tummy, but you love your nose, focus on your nose only. Now know that the world will see you as you see yourself. Every time you look in the mirror, allow your eyes to gravitate only to those areas you appreciate. You are exceptional; see yourself as you truly are. How you see yourself is how others will see you. You want your man to see all the beauty you are—you want to show yourself so he recognizes you are an exceptional woman.

Crown Jewel: Whatever you focus on gets bigger. The more you focus on positive areas, the more they grow. It's positive reinforcement.

In life, you get what you focus on. You get what you look for. Literally, what you focus on is brought into your conscious awareness. Try this exercise where you are right now: open your eyes wide and look for everything blue in sight, then close your eyes. Can you remember what was red? Now open your eyes and discover what is red that originally you glanced right over because your focus was only on blue. I use this in my life to look for positive reinforcement. I focus only on the people and things that support my happiness and personal growth.

This principle holds true in all of life. Think about when you bought your car. Now, does it seem as if there are millions of your exact car on the road? It's not because everyone ran out and bought it after you did. It's the fact that you now focus on those automobiles. It was brought into your conscious awareness. You get what you look for; you get what you focus on. By focusing your attention on the type of car you now have, you become more aware of that car. Without even noticing that you are doing it, unconsciously, your attention is now more aware and brings those cars to your conscious attention. Your unconscious mind is constantly looking for patterns; your unconscious is constantly trying to figure out how things relate to you. It's like someone in a crowded space yelling "Hey you" and everyone looks to see if they are the object of the words; or seeing an advertisement on television and wondering how you would look or feel if you used that product. I will discuss much more on the power of the unconscious mind in Chapter 11. By understanding the unconscious mind, which is not under the direct control of the conscious mind, you can control it in indirect ways.

Crown Jewel: Your unconscious mind is constantly trying to figure out how things relate to you. It is obedient and only works to serve you, so it gives you whatever you look for—you get what you look for.

Practice on yourself and become aware of how you can control your power of focus to appreciate even more of your exceptional gifts internally as well as externally. The same goes for him. If you focus on his negatives, they get bigger. If you focus on his positives, they get bigger. The more you appreciate and rejoice in all the exceptional qualities within him, the more those qualities will expand. Whatever you look for, you will find. Look for all the gifts he has to offer. He will grow those attributes even stronger with your support. This is why you always hear, "Behind every good man is a good woman." Even if he is not your exceptional man, bless him with your support in allowing him to flourish into the most exceptional man he can be, so he might attract that woman who is his match. Let it be your objective to leave people better than you found them. Encourage his growth and your own by choosing your words carefully. There is incredible power in words; words are transmuted into emotion.

The Power of Words—A Word to the Wise

The quality of our lives is a direct reflection of the feelings we experience. The feelings we experience are a direct reflection of the words we use to describe those experiences. We label an experience with words; the specific words we choose then elicit a feeling in us towards that experience. Don't just take my word for it; try it. The next time someone asks you how you are, don't say the typical "Good." Choose a new word. Mine is "Fantastic." If you would normally say you are having an okay day, say you are having a "Terrific day." If you would normally define yourself as happy, call your mood "Ecstatic." Watch the response you get from men on the street, then notice your own feelings after seeing how your new energy level affects others. People are usually wowed by my "Fantastic" reply. Now that I really do feel fantastic, I say it with even more gusto. The feedback I get from them brings my energy up even more. Use your words to increase the intensity of your positive emotions.

Crown Jewel: The meaning we place on a situation determines the words we use to describe that situation; change your words and you change the meaning.

You can change the way you feel about a situation by changing the words you assign to describe the experience. The following list of *Words to Enhance Positive Emotions* will assist you in expanding your positive vocabulary, whether written or spoken, internally or externally. Choose your words wisely, for the power of your words is mightier than the sword. If you begin to repeatedly incorporate this positive language into your daily speech patterns, it will become second nature, and the words will be your automatic response language. What man isn't attracted to happy, positive women? I have practiced using many of these words for several years, and now when I describe things, I rarely use the word "good" because I am so used to describing things as wonderful, fantastic, and extraordinary. "Good" doesn't even come up as an emotion for me. It seems to me that "good" these days feels more like mediocre. These new words I use are so much more colorful and fun to speak. They make me feel exceptional whether I'm reading them, speaking them, or feeling them. I can't help but get excited.

Words to Enhance Positive Emotions:

Exceptional, extraordinary, jubilant, fabulous, fantastic, spectacular, wonderful, super, lively, loving, grateful, supercalifragilisticexpialidocious, fulfilled, happy, gregarious, joyful, confident, exciting, smart, intelligent, courageous, thoughtful, supportive, nurturing, outstanding, caring, encouraging, phenomenal, blissful, amazing, fantastic, wonderful, elated, outstanding, unbelievable, ecstatic, exuberant, energized, spectacular, monumental, serene, impassioned, tremendous, awesome, blessed, vivacious, excellent, dynamite, magical, exhilarated, incredible, enthralled, captivated, enraptured, unstoppable, relish, exuding, compelled, focused, explosive, brilliant, gorgeous, outstanding, unbelievable, enchanting, enticing, witty, funny, meaningful, passionate, momentous, impressive, striking, scrumptious, delicious, pleasurable, exhilarating, awesome, exalted, grandiose, grand, imperial, magnificent, marvelous, majestic, mind-blowing, monumental, noble, out of this world, regal, sumptuous, sublime, superb, dainty, delicate, elegant, exclusive, first-class, grand, luscious, lush, luxuriant, opulent, posh, angelic, alluring, admirable, beauteous, charming, classy, cute, dazzling, delicate, delightful, divine, exquisite, fascinating, foxy, graceful, handsome, ideal, lovely, magnificent, pleasing, pretty, radiant, ravishing, refined, resplendent, shapely, splendid, statuesque, stunning, invincible, abundant, fortunate, treasure, triumph, rejoice, enthusiasm, astounding, astonishing, adorable, sensational, inspirational, whimsical, precious, amusing, playful, cherish, and supreme.

The same works on negative emotions. If you are under an immense amount of stress and someone asks you about it, try calling it a "challenge" or a "perplexing situation" instead. If you're totally depressed, try defining it as a "little down." If you're feeling lonely, define it as "available." Find yourself "slightly concerned" rather than "scared." It will immediately begin to feel like less of an obstacle. If you are having a fight or an argument with someone, immediately change your terminology to a "difference of opinion." "Interesting" is a great word to lessen any negative emotion. Before you allow your mind to immediately judge a situation, use the word "interesting" to allow the brain a moment to process the information rather than judge it as bad or good. For example, instead of thinking of an event as a disaster, reassess the situation as "interesting." Say you get a flat tire. Instead of going into a panic, judge the situation as "interesting." Then, once the flat tire is an interesting situation, maybe you can learn how to put on a spare or meet an interesting new hero who will help you fix it. You can reevaluate the situation, allowing it to become of service to you, making your life better and yourself better for having had the experience. Don't take my word for it; try it. Changing the words you use to define a situation will change the way you feel in your body toward what is occurring.

Crown Jewel: Anytime you are having a struggle or difficulty, redefine it as a "challenging" or an "interesting" situation.

"There is nothing either good or bad, but thinking makes it so."[1] (William Shakespeare) It is how we define events and conditions that brings the meaning to those events and conditions. Nothing has any meaning except the meaning we give it. The things that "happen to us" are based on our translation of an experience into words. It is our "interpretation of reality." Don't be an unconscious victim. In any situation you get to choose the meaning you assign it. The meaning you attach to events and conditions determines the quality of your life. The same is true of tangible things. The meaning you attach to an object represents that object and its significance to you. People tend to judge by asking, "Is it good or bad?" or, "Is it right or wrong?" Instead ask, "What's the meaning?" Extricate from your mind all the preconceived judgments you have developed throughout the years. Figure out how a situation serves you. Determine "What's the lesson?"

Crown Jewel: Anytime you have a challenging or interesting situation present itself, ask, "What's the meaning?" and then, "What's the lesson?"

Words to Lessen Negative Emotions:

Challenged, delayed, baffled, surprised, aware, stimulated, available, misunderstood, unresourceful, uneasy, different, learning, curious, fascinated, anticipating, misinterpreted, busy, in demand, many opportunities, perplexing; interesting, a little down, slightly concerned, difference of opinion, puzzled, enlightened, clarified, amazed, perturbed, peeved, flustered, mystified, peculiar, and ruffled.

The same is true when you speak internally to yourself—carefully choose the language you use. This internal speech also includes the questions you ask yourself. Do you constantly beat yourself up? Do you never think you are good enough? Do you ask yourself, "Why is this happening to me?" or, "Why doesn't he like me?" Ask a better question, whether of yourself or of others, and you will get a better answer. I always go back to, "What's the lesson?" It takes the sting out and gives meaning to any experience. Your habitual vocabulary will determine your primary emotions. What is your habitual vocabulary saying about you? Literally, what are the words saying? Those habitual emotions will determine the quality of your life. People tend to feel the same experience differently in their bodies by virtue of the different language they use to describe an event. Words attach meaning to any given experience, which becomes our reality of that experience, regardless of whether it's objectively accurate.

Crown Jewel: People act based on their emotions and then back up their decisions with logical reasoning.

Whatever experience you think of over and over, your body feels as if it were occurring in reality over and over again. Your mind thinks in pictures. The pictures running through your head are as real to your body as the original experience — even if you literally create the pictures from thin air. I know you have all done the lemon trick, but for the sake of experiment, let's test it again. Think of biting into a big, yellow, super-sour lemon. Really see it, then smell it, then taste it. Does your mouth start salivating at the thought? Your mind reacts to sensory suggestions, even those presented through written words.

After a person has an initial experience with a sight, sound, taste, touch, or smell, the mere mention of that experience can immediately evoke the original sensory response. Have you ever had an experience where you smell something baking or hear a certain song that takes you back in time and evokes the feelings from long ago? Your stored memories are attached to sensory response. If you focus on a negative experience, then you experience it over and over in your body. Whatever emotions we experience are a direct result of the quality of our attention to our thoughts. You can choose to recall old thoughts or create new thoughts; your mind doesn't know the difference from the real memory versus the imagined thought. Choose to direct your thoughts to those positive experiences that will serve you and make your amazing life even more extraordinary. This positive exuberance will be captured in your profile to come. You go, goddess.

Crown Jewel: Your mind thinks in pictures. Guilt is self-persecution because you keep repeating the negative experience over and over in your mind; with every memory, the feelings in your body are as real as the original experience.

Chapter Five:

Completing Your Online Profile

You—yes, you—are an exceptional woman. Let your inner beauty emanate online. You are a unique being with sensational gifts and talents like no other before you. In completing your profile, as in connecting with others in general, it is most important to put your best foot forward. Most people know more about their limitations than their assets. You are who you think you are. In order to present all your exceptional qualities to others, you must know all the exceptional qualities you possess. If you have trouble seeing what is right in front of you, look in the mirror. If you still have trouble, ask your friends. Oftentimes others see our gifts more clearly than we do ourselves. Two heads are always better than one. They are sure to know all your exceptional qualities and may assist you in your personal recognition of your true essence. Even ask a stranger or two. Sometimes an individual who has no preconceived notion of us can see past the illusion we create to a depth we have yet to discover. The impartial witness may detect those deep-seated qualities longing to be expressed, so we might meet our full potential.

Men, and women, too, are attracted to confidence in a significant partner. Confidence in our man is super sexy, isn't it? Confidence is king and your king most certainly is confident. It's so appealing when he looks and acts like he knows exactly what he is doing. You know he's got your back. Individuals who lack confidence tend to over-analyze everything—every situation poses a threat. That stress is internalized as negative thoughts, which inevitably lead to negative actions. People with low self-worth are hypersensitive and self-critical, never realizing the value in themselves or in a challenging experience. They haven't yet learned to ask, "What's the lesson?" All these lessons have allowed you to become your greatest resource. Since you now know you are your greatest resource and all you need is within you, you can simply determine how to outsource any given obstacle. It's just like hiring a plumber. You may not know how to fix the sink, but you know how to hire someone who can.

Crown Jewel: Confidence is sexy. Just as you practice your smile from the outside in, build your self-esteem before you speak a word.

The wisdom you have attained over the course of your life has gotten you this far—what a remarkable job you have done. Let your self-assured mannerisms show in the way you stand, the way you move your body, the way you speak. Let it exude from every pore of your being. Science now tells us the mind is not only in the brain; memory is held in every cell of your body. Let every cell radiate that confidence you have taken a lifetime of experiences to acquire. No crazy insecurity about things that have yet to exist. No daydreaming about negatives—only positives. Allow this confidence to flow out onto the screen through your profile and spill out into all areas of your life.

Your profile may consist of photos, a user name, a user tagline or caption, automated questions, and/or a section to express who you are and who you are looking for. Your primary photo and your user name are the first things other members see. Capture his attention and define yourself with creative gems. Your user name instantly represents you. It is your first marketing tool; it should be creative and unique, just like you. Look for something that identifies who you are and what you enjoy in a clever way. To brainstorm for your user name, write out a list of adjectives and then a list of nouns describing you. Then combine two, and ta-da. It's done. You could even use a third word from your lists, space permitting. Check to see how many characters the site designates for user names. I opted for three nouns; my user name is SmilesSassClass—it describes me to a "T". Notice my use of capital letters.

In your user name, as in all areas of creating a profile, you always, always want to be extremely upbeat and positive.

Most sites allow for the use of numbers as well as characters, but too many numbers can become confusing. Sexually suggestive names will get you a completely different category of men than those with no innuendo.

Think about the type of exceptional man you're attempting to attract. Entice him into your profile by making him want to explore you further.

Much like your user name, let your tagline grab his attention. Make it clever, funny, even philosophical if that feels right. You want to avoid choosing an overused cliché or phrase. Examples of frequently used terms or words are "Looking for love?" "Are you out there?" "Looking for Mr. Right?" "Pick Me Pick Me," "Looking for a partner in crime," "Searching for my soul mate," "I'm what you're looking for," "Must love dogs," "You've found your better half," "Take a chance," and "Hello, Hey, and Hi." Surf the site and view other members' taglines to stimulate your thought process and avoid overused ideas. Think of it as a title to an autobiography you are writing to be published. Keep in mind: you are exceptional and want to convey that to your audience. You want to draw the member in to read more. Again, always keep your tone super positive. Check to see how many characters the site permits for headings, and make certain the entire tagline can be read even if you have not *opened* the profile. Sometimes the tagline will reveal only a specific number of characters until you open up the profile, at which time all the characters are shown. If there is a limit to the characters shown before the profile is open, keep the tagline within that limit so it may be fully read even if the profile is NOT open. I suggest a catchy, short tagline.

Crown Jewel: Surf the site to read profiles of both men and women to brainstorm and avoid overused phrases.

Sites may have you answer a series of questions to ascertain your personality traits, relationship preferences, and your requirements in a partner. This information will define your location, the proximity in which you are pursuing mates, relationship status, age, height, body type, eyes, hair, smoking habits, drinking habits, political views, education, occupation, income, relationship status, children, pets, ethnicity, faith, astrological sign, languages spoken, hobbies, and interests. These questions alone go much deeper than a typical first date. Again, look at the time value. Oftentimes men searching do not read all or even some of my profile and will message irrespective as to whether they are suitable according to my preferences listed in my profile. While it is true that some do not read profiles, you want every part of your profile to represent the exceptional woman you are because chances are your exceptional man does read the profiles.

The Autobiographical Section of Your Profile

You are a radiant jewel. Your online profile should captivate your audience. The self-expressed, autobiographical portion of your profile is your written words rather than automated questions. A great autobiographical section takes only 250-400 words. It's the quality of those words that's most important. Check the site to determine the minimum and maximum characters permitted. This is going to be a breeze for you because you know yourself better than anyone, and actually, you don't want your profile too long. If it is lengthy, it will cause men to skim over it quickly. Most online daters are looking at numerous profiles every day, and if it's an overwhelming read, he may just pass it by. Tailor it distinctively to yourself and keep it interesting. You don't want to sound generic like, "I'm a great girl," or, "I'm funny." Do not use the typical vernacular of the online dating scene, making yourself sound common. Let him see *how* you are a great girl or *why* you are funny in the context of your profile. Focus on what will give him a better understanding of you and show the magnificence of who you are.

Crown Jewel: Don't write, "I'm a great girl," or, "I'm funny" in your profile. Demonstrate those qualities creatively. Review my profile and the example profiles in Chapter 16 for brainstorming ideas.

In describing yourself in the autobiographical free-for-all section, remember you are exceptional. Let every man online and in the world know it. Close your eyes and remember the most exceptional things you have accomplished in your life. Where were you? What happened? Who was with you? How did you feel? What did you say? Visualize that exact moment in your mind and experience the feelings you felt when you achieved your ultimate goal. Now recall another exceptional accomplishment, and another, and another. Flood yourself with these monumental memories so you are overflowing with gratitude for yourself and all you have achieved in your life. Wow, have you accomplished some outstanding goals and what a remarkable woman you are today. All the knowledge you have compiled throughout your life has kept you on your path to becoming the exceptional woman you offer the world. Now is the time to share all those gifts you harbor. Your gifts, your talents, your soul make you an exceptional woman. And your exceptional man is looking for just that—your exceptional man is looking for you.

Crown Jewel: "Our deepest fear is not that we are inadequate. Our deepest fear is that we are powerful beyond measure. It is our light, not our darkness that most frightens us."2 (Marianne Williamson)

Let your future mate know the full package he is getting with you. Not in an arrogant way, but in a loving way filled with honor for all the tremendous talents you are able to share. No one in the world is special in the ways you are. Not another soul on earth can offer your particular talents. No one else can offer the exact contribution that is your life's purpose. Let that core energy burning from within out to play. Let your dynamic spirit radiate off the page. The charisma you display in your profile will be alluring. Always, always use positive language. We all get frustrated with dating and life in general. We all face challenges, but this is not the place to vent those frustrations. You are looking for your ideal man. He is a positive, exceptional man looking for a positive, exceptional woman. You get what you are, not what you want. Water seeks its own level. It's the law of cause and effect. We will cover this in more detail in Chapter 17. Truly be that positive, exceptional woman you already are. Like attracts like. It's magnetic—whatever you are, or have, you attract more of.

Don't use any needy or desperate language like "looking for my soul mate" or "searching for my knight in shining armor." You are full from the inside out—you want a real relationship with a real man. These cliché terms make it appear you are looking for something intangible, a fairy tale no man could live up to. Never, never use any negative language or references in your profile. Take note of the use of language in a man's profile as well. I quite commonly read these negative statements: "I can't believe I'm on here," "Look like your pictures," "I'm not into games," and "I'm not willing to settle." These make it seem the user is hurt from old experiences. I always evaluate a man's vocabulary to see if it is positive or negative; it gives me an indication of how he lives his life. It is often said, "How you do anything, is how you do everything." A person's profile is a reflection of the core energy of that person. You must release any bitterness and frustration from the past. You're not punishing your old flame by harboring those feelings of resentment; you're punishing yourself. You are a joyful, lively soul yearning to contribute your gifts. You don't carry any baggage, only lessons inspiring your evolution into the exceptional woman you are. Give those exceptional men a glimpse of the dazzling beauty you are inside.

Crown Jewel: Whether with pen and paper, on the phone, or in person, at every opportunity always express yourself in a positive, positive way.

In my personal profile, I used my creativity to come up with a unique way to describe myself; see below. If you notice, I did not write about what I do or don't want in a partner. With the magnitude of users online, people are screening in or out immediately, and I don't want to be ruled out for anything that could be misconstrued. Online dating offers hundreds of thousands of prospective partners, so inevitably members will develop a rapid-fire process of elimination and I don't want to be shot down for anything that's not a "must." Keep this in mind when writing your profile. I prefer having men communicate with me, reviewing their profile, and then determining if I am interested, rather than having them rule me out because of something I have stated I am expressly looking for. When you are evaluating eligible men, eliminate only for good cause, not just to clear your inbox. Automated questions offer only two-dimensional information while human beings are multidimensional masterpieces. The written words of a profile are just one bit of data in the information gathering process.

I had a blast creating my online profile using one of my favorite outlets in life to describe myself, music. I carefully selected songs that describe my personality traits and then songs that don't represent me. I used the contrast of the two in a fun, playful way. Everyone loves music; it's a vivid, colorful way to engage the mind. I went on to explain a little about how I see the world and relationships so that men could get a deeper sense of who I am in my heart. Notice the positive and upbeat tone of the profile. I spent a few hours creating my profile; really paying attention to detail to make it a wonderful representation of who I am. Thousands, if not millions of men could view my profile—it was well worth the investment of time and energy. The following is the autobiographical excerpt from my actual profile.

Songs that describe me –

Honesty_____I Don't Want to Go to Rehab;

Glamorous_____Smells Like Teen Spirit;

Carolina Girl_____She's a Super Freak;

Unforgettable_____The Lady is a Tramp;

Dancing Queen_____Your Cheatin' Heart;

R-E-S-P-E-C-T_____Fat Bottomed Girls;

Good Vibrations_____Comfortably Numb;

Born to Be Wild_____Suspicious Minds;

Brown Eyed Girl_____Jailhouse Rock;

American Woman_____Heart of Stone;

Daydream Believer_____Material Girl;

Don't Stop Believin_____Devil Inside;

Always a Woman to Me_____Too Shy;

Girls Just Wanna Have Fun_____Crazy;

I believe many people spend their lives looking for meaning, focusing on the negative rather than the positive. My cup isn't just half-full, it's overflowing. I am continually striving for excellence in everything I do and am willing to work hard in order to achieve the ultimate results. I love to learn and experience new adventures. I also love to laugh. I am outside the box—I don't think or behave like the average person. I can assimilate to people from all walks of life—from your favorite NASCAR driver to your most revered political figure. I love people and love life. I am looking for a man to be a man. I am not submissive, but I am extremely feminine and want a man that is not. I believe a relationship is not a place to get something, but a place to give something. I feel the purpose of relationships is to magnify human emotion. I believe the test of a relationship is who you become around the person.

Keep in mind your target audience: you are writing to capture your exceptional man's attention. You want your profile to be as complete an expression of yourself as you are able to put into words. You want it to show your intellect as well as your playful side. This one document will be used as your application over and over to introduce you to possible suitors. Think of creating your profile as creating a dating resume. You have to do the work only once, and it will reach thousands of potentials. You get back the energy you put out. Be at your peak emotional state to prepare for the task at hand. The best gentleman's profile I ever read was in the form of a letter to God requesting his future bride—he was an atheist. It was clever and laid out who he was and what he was looking for in a relationship. You don't want to appear common in your profile because you aren't—you are the only one of you there will ever be. You are EXCEPTIONAL.

Crown Jewel: Take all the time and energy you need to create your online profile. Think of your profile as your dating resume—you have to do the work only once, and it will reach thousands of potentials.

Be inventive, like when you were a child coming up with stories in your head. Put a pen to paper and see where it leads you. Browse the Internet to stimulate your thought process. Examine other profiles of men and women to brainstorm. Take note of what you like and don't like. Then, as I did in writing this book, sit down and write. It will flow from you if you put in the time and effort. If you really are blocked and unable to do it yourself, hire someone or ask a friend to help. It's worth the investment when you're talking about finding that exceptional man to share your life with. You can sit down with a professional writer and collaborate on your profile. This isn't school; you're not cheating. The best writers in the world have editors to help them. Not once on a date or even in a message have I been in asked if I wrote my profile—which I did. Your pictures will grab his attention, and your words will seal the deal because you are an exceptional woman.

Exceptional Talents (words to stimulate your writing):

Philanthropy, Charitable Events, Volunteering, Renovations, Antiques, Networking, Gardening, Landscaping, Crafts, Collecting, Chess, Magic, Museums, Exploring New Areas, Learning New Things, Nightclubs, Restaurants, Cooking, Wine Tasting, Astrology, Astronomy, Religion, Spirituality, Meditation, Shopping, Travel, Camping, Sightseeing, Reading, Writing, Movies, Television, Conferences, Decorating, Design, Painting, Drawing, Illustration, Comics, Mosaics, Printmaking, Fine Art, Calligraphy, Photography, Mixed Media, Sculpture, Conceptual Art, Architecture, Fashion, Instruments, Music, Theater, Film, Musicals, Free Form Dancing, Ballet, Tap, Jazz, Salsa, Miranga, Hip Hop, Belly Dance, Ball Room, Tango, Waltz, Swing, Shag; Fire Sports (eating/dancing), Roller Skating, Inline Skating, Ice Skating, Skiing, Bowling, Archery, Target Shooting, Golf, Fencing, Walking, Running, Cycling, Hiking, Rock Climbing, Kayaking, Canoeing, Sailing, Rowing, Swimming, Surfing, Windsurfing, Kite Boarding, Boating, Fishing, Snorkeling, Scuba Diving, Wrestling, Boxing, Weights, Yoga, Acrobatics, Gymnastics, Pilates, Taekwondo, Judo, Equestrian, Dog Sledding, Bobsleighing, Soccer, Football, Rugby, Hockey, Basketball, Volleyball, Handball, Tennis, Ping Pong, and Badminton, Cultures (eating/studying/traveling) - British, Irish, Scottish, French, Swiss, German, Italian, Spanish, Greek, Austrian, Romanian, British, Russian, Swedish, Lebanese, Turkish, Persian, South African, Moroccan,

Egyptian, Australian, New Zealand, Japanese, Chinese, Thai, Vietnamese, Indonesian, Korean, Mongolian, Indian, Canadian, Mexican, Jamaican, Chilean, Peruvian, Brazilian, Columbian.

Crown Jewel: To some people, spelling and grammatical errors are huge pet peeves. You don't want to be ruled out for something so insignificant. So proofread, proofread, proofread.

Chapter Six:

Choosing Your Online Profile Photos

We all know men are visual creatures. Men typically fall in love through their eyes, while women typically fall in love through their ears. That's not to say one is right and one is wrong. Every man wants to connect and get along on a fundamental level with his partner, but he is first guided by his visual attraction. That's why you must put your best face forward. You're a gorgeous individual unlike any other on earth; bring forth that confidence you have nurtured. Let your prospects see you radiate off the screen. Spend the effort, spend the time, and spend the money to look and feel your best. Get new clothes, hire a makeup artist, spend a day at the hair salon, enjoy a mani/pedi. Let the stunning, unique beauty you are be seen.

Crown Jewel: Want whiter teeth? Five-minute teeth whitener gel is available at any drug store. It's only a couple of dollars and will make those pearly whites sparkle even more. Consult with your dentist as to what is right for you.

Have fun with it, and then take professional photos. Let me emphasize the importance of hiring a makeup artist and/or hair stylist and a professional photographer. There is a reason all the top models, actresses, and other celebrities do it. Professional photographers work with professional equipment in studios with lighting engineered just for that purpose. They know precisely which lens to use in what light. The lighting and angles make all the difference in how the portrait turns out on paper and on screen. In photography you must capture depths artistically since physically pictures are only two-dimensional. The illusion of depth perception in an image is created through the use of angles and lighting. High-end photographers use professional-caliber cameras, lenses, lighting, and accessories. They know the camera's nuances and all the photographic techniques to make you look your best. You want your portrait to be natural and put you in the best possible light, literally. Just look at your personal photos. Are there some you love and some you hate? What made the difference? They were all really you.

When I joined the online dating scene, I used photos of myself that I thought were pretty good. I got decent responses on my profile, but then I decided to have a professional photo shoot, and WOW. The photos were stunning. They still looked exactly like me, just accentuating all my positives. The messages started flooding in by the droves, and the number of winks/pokes/nudge/DMs and emails dramatically increased. Not only did the amount of attention I was getting substantially increase, but the potential of those men did as well. The men were more in line with the qualities I was looking for in a lifetime partner. At first, I was slightly nervous; since the photos were so beautiful, my dates would think it was a bait and switch. But when they see me in person, some feel the need to comment that I look "better in person."

Crown Jewel: The better the quality of your profile, the better the quality of the gentlemen responding.

Discuss with your photographer where you intend to use your new photos. Generally, photographers own all copyrights to the images they create, and they issue licenses enabling you to reproduce images for a certain duration of time or "in perpetuity," which means forever. After your license period ends, this right reverts back to them so they may reuse the images. What this means to you is that the photographer will grant you a license to use your photos in an agreed-upon media (website, business cards, etc.) for an agreed-upon term. A photographer is not entitled to use your photos for commercial use without your express permission in writing. You want to have the terms agreed upon in writing to protect you both. Laws and rights vary by state; consult with an attorney regarding any release you are asked to sign or wish to receive.

Every photo shoot and TV set has a professional makeup artist, a professional hairdresser, and a professional wardrobe stylist on staff. Typically, in order to save time and money, you can use one multitalented individual for all these services. The makeup you put on for photos is vastly different from makeup applied off camera. Professionals are trained in the science of color and makeup application. Through highlighting, contouring, and placement, the artist can create the illusion of perfect bone structure and balance all your features perfectly. It is truly an artist "painting a face." The makeup artist will assess your skin pigmentation, eye and hair shades, and outfit colors to determine the best shades and shaping of your features. The artist will take into account indoor versus outdoor lighting and even the type of lens the photographer uses. You should always interview a makeup artist in advance and request to review his or her portfolio, and I would go so far as to request a test run. If you don't know where to find a makeup artist and/or hair stylist, ask your photographer for guidance. It's usually a tight industry, and your photographer should know whom to refer you to.

Think glamour magazines, not glamour shots. You want elegance with a hint of sex appeal. Sex appeal doesn't have to be skin. You want him to clearly see you are a feminine woman, not a sex kitten. A look, a feeling emoting from your photos will set the tone. Let me reiterate: the most important part of your profile is the pictures. You want these pictures to show your authentic self in the best possible light. You are a unique beauty with exceptional qualities a professional will know how to expose in your photos. A professional makeup artist will know how to amplify your physical features making you radiant on camera. A professional photographer will know how to use the camera to best accentuate those qualities. No matter how much energy and time you must expend, or how much money you must part with, it's worth it to find your exceptional man.

Crown Jewel: Large pupils are more attractive. Pupils grow to let more light in, so in dim light they are bigger, while in bright light they are smaller. Close your eyes and don't cast your eyes directly into a bright light before the shot.

If you are adamantly opposed to hiring a photographer or just plain don't have the funds, don't fret. I have tips that will allow your shoots to reveal the exquisite beauty you are no matter who is snapping your shots. Even if you are going to hire a professional photographer, all these tips are great for practice warm-ups. Get creative; you have friends. One of them is bound to be skillful with a camera, and another is sure to know an editing program such as Photoshop. If not, check your local college or community school's arts/photography program. Plenty of students are eager for experience. These same tips are great for hair and makeup talent as well. Check your local cosmetology school. Most of these schools cut and color for very minimal charges, and an instructor will closely supervise the work. At many cosmetic stores and counters, if you spend a specified minimum on cosmetics, a professional will apply your full makeup free of charge. With many of the makeup artists at these stores, you can even schedule an appointment in advance of your photo shoot.

Crown Jewel: Wear fake lashes for your photos. They won't look fake on camera, but they will TOTALLY amplify your positives. Extra hairpieces can give you the fullness or length you've always wanted.

You Don't have to be a Model to Look Like One

There is a reason they call it a *model*. You don't have to reinvent the wheel here. Look at all the latest magazines. Study the makeup, the hair, the outfits, and the poses. Pretend it's research for a book report in school. Do the homework. It's like anything in life—others have gone before you. Learn from their processes and adapt them to fit your needs. With any goal you have, you can model the best in that field. If you inundate yourself with the same techniques they used and do exactly what they do, you will find your excellence. What makes a professional achieve a higher result? Determination and practice, practice, practice. Examine magazines for sample poses. Practice posing in front of the mirror. Even practice shooting with girlfriends. The fun part with this one is that you can actually practice all these techniques with your colleagues at work, with your girlfriends, and even on real dates. It's like playing dress-up when you were little.

Being naturally beautiful doesn't necessarily translate into being photogenic. Photography is two-dimensional, so you lose depth perception, which may make you appear less or more attractive. This two-dimensionality also causes you to look wider, hence the idea that the camera adds ten pounds. Being photogenic is about knowing how to posture yourself and express your charisma in front of the camera. Models spend countless hours over years learning this expertise. They know how to precisely position their bodies while at the same time being comfortable in their own skin. Act natural, breathe, and relax; you want the photo to reflect who you really are, not a stiff, rigid subject. Use the real smile—not just the mouth; incorporate the eyes and the entire face. Visualize happy, even funny times. A smile is best if it comes from the inside out. Imagine the camera is your best friend. Really visually imagine it is a girlfriend you are talking to and playing with. Dance with delight internally and let your bliss pour out through your eyes. Let your eyes sparkle more than the most brilliant cut gemstone. Don't look directly at the camera; look through it.

Crown Jewel: Don't clench your teeth. Shake your jaw out. Literally wiggle your bottom jaw from left to right, up and down to relieve any tension. Rest your tongue on the roof of your mouth.

No one has a perfectly symmetrical body. Research shows we find people more attractive with more symmetrical features. To camouflage any asymmetry, slightly angle your face toward the camera. Whatever's closest to the camera appears larger. If one of your eyes is smaller, lean slightly toward the camera with that side of your face. Raise your eyebrows a little for more definition. Your arms always look bigger than they are because they're slightly in front of the rest of you, hence closer to the camera. If you lean into the camera, it makes the head look slightly bigger; therefore, the arms seem smaller. Photography is two-dimensional so it allows us to work with the camera and make adjustments to change the dynamics of what is actually being photographed. You can use your brainpower to model those who have the perfect poses down. Supermodels know the tricks of the trade—and now you will too.

The horizontal pose can make you appear wider, while the classic model pose shows curves and simulates a narrower waistline. We know how men love curves. Mae West defined a "Curve: The loveliest distance between two points." To avoid a double chin, place your head slightly forward, but don't overdo it and look like an ostrich. To accentuate femininity, try a slight downward and tilted head, revealing a hint of the neck. Hold your arms slightly out from your body or place one on your hip. This shows your definition rather than smooshing the skin of your arms against your chest. Watch your posture—no slouching. Pretend you have a string that pulls you up from the crown of your head, making your spine erect. Stretch out to elongate your body and to avoid wrinkling or smooshing skin. Pull your shoulders back and down, elongating the neck while pulling your chest forward, and gently suck in your stomach—if you overdo this, it will look like it.

Crown Jewel: Never stand fully facing the camera. The following classic model pose makes everyone look better:

> ➢ First: Arrange your body three-quarters (forty-five degrees) toward the camera.

> ➢ Second: Stand with one foot in front of the other, toes pointing toward the camera.

> ➢ Third: Rest all your weight on your back leg, with the front leg slightly bent.

> ➢ Fourth: Turn at the waist, squaring your shoulders to the camera, with one shoulder a bit closer to the camera.

If you put one part of your body on anything, just superficially touch it. Don't apply any weight; it gives that smooshing effect. If you apply any pressure, it distorts the natural shape and form of your skin. For example, if you rest your head on your hand or your arm on a table, literally just graze the surface—do not press down. Most people "freeze" for the camera and stiffen every muscle, which shows as tension throughout every muscle in their body. Your face alone has forty-three muscles. Before that photo is snapped, shake your body out, and then pose. Don't freeze externally, becoming inflexible and rigid. Don't freeze internally, holding your heart and breath. Literally jump up and down and shake every inch of your body, from your toes to your ears, to relieve pent-up tension. Let your light and love show in every speck of your being. Remember to keep breathing.

It seems everyone wants to look thinner for the camera. Here are fashion secrets that make it easy. Wear a spandex body-shaping undergarment to hold everything tightly in place. These smooth out any lumps, making you appear slimmer and more curvaceous. Well-fitting clothes are the most flattering. A tailored jacket can define your curves while hiding lumps and bumps. Simple, straight-leg pants with no pockets or embellishments make you look thinner. A knee-length skirt with straight lines or an A-line will create the look of longer legs; full skirts will add pounds. Pumps always make your legs appear longer and more shapely. Heels add height, so by default you always look slimmer. To remain balanced in heels a woman must have erect posture; this upright stance actually adds height as well. Nude heels are a must; they give you that extra height and don't cut you off at the ankle. Dressing in one color from head to toe, particularly in dark colors, will make you look more slender. Patterns can be too busy for the camera. Digital cameras have difficulties with black, white, and red, which can produce too much contrast.

Crown Jewel: Photos should always be taken from above. Photos taken from below add that infamous ten pounds.

You don't have to look like a supermodel to be gorgeous. Universally, the traits men consider most beautiful in women are extremely feminine qualities. Men like the polarity of the sexes and want to see the obvious differences in women. All those distinctive traits, even the ones you may not like, make you the magnificent beauty you are. There is a reason it is said "Beauty is in the eye of the beholder." Some men love flat woman with a top open down to there, some men love women with big rumps with tight pants, some men love women with gaps between their two front teeth, some men love women with moles, some love straight hair, some curly, some love brunettes, others blondes—no matter what your type, an exceptional man is looking for exactly you. It's like selling a house. Not everybody wants the same things in a house, and you need to find only one buyer. One client may not buy the house because the bedroom is on the first floor, but the next may buy it only because the bedroom is on the first floor. Don't be afraid to show your best you, in the best possible light. Unleash your femininity. Smile and enjoy the process. You were created to meet your full potential. Never settle for less. You are gorgeous from the inside out.

Your photos get your exceptional man in the door. Your soul keeps him. You are an extraordinary woman. You are a gift to the world. For your profile, choose four or five of your new professional photos in different outfits and poses. Mix in a couple nonprofessional great shots of you. Never, never have pictures with your friends or an ex-boyfriend and black out faces. Pictures with pets and children distract the attention from you. Scenic pictures without you in them, even those of travel destinations should be avoided. Make certain your photos don't reveal any personal information; for instance where you work or live. Never, never have lingerie or other extremely suggestive shots. You are a classy, exceptional woman, and that's what your photos will expose. The photographer is only going to bring out your natural beauty, not change who you are. When your date sees you in person, you will be just what he has expected because he already has the picture in his head. Later, in Chapter 9 I describe precisely how to prepare for a date, and in Chapter 19 I give makeup tips to magnify those positives.

Crown Jewel: Keep in mind he may read things into the surroundings in your images, so be particular with what you expose. You will be looking at the surroundings in his pictures to gain insight as well.

Let's face it: we are dating online because we are true romantics. We are in love with the idea of falling in love with our ideal mate. He is out there, and yes, he is a needle in a haystack. Use the metal detector to find him. These photos will be the magnet, and he will not be able to resist your pull. The energy you radiate will be captured in these priceless photos and bring you to your destiny—so no skimping. How long have you been looking for your exceptional man? How many ways have you attempted to find him? How much time and money have you put into those efforts? Beautiful photos are a much better investment than a couple of drinks at a bar waiting for an acceptable man to stumble in. These pictures will not only be of benefit in finding your exceptional man; rest assured you can use them in other areas of your life. Think social media such as Facebook, Instagram, and LinkedIn. All your friends will get to share your exquisite new images. Now that you have fantastic photos and a prolific profile, men will be vying for your attention, and you have but to choose which are of interest.

Chapter Seven:

How to Identify Your Exceptional Man

Here is the greatest thing about online dating: you are the judge. You can assess all the information provided and determine if you choose to engage a man further. When you screen his profile, pay close attention to every seemingly little detail. Do his positions on children and religion match yours? Are his drinking and smoking habits acceptable? Examine what he reads and his hobbies; are those of interest to you? Are his favorite things important to you, too? The family that plays together stays together. Common values and beliefs are fundamental to a strong relationship. Look at both his exercise routine and his body type to see if they are consistent with what you desire in a partner. Is his political stance reasonable to you? Is there an educational level you must have in a mate? Yes, it's true: some have been known to lie on their profiles, but if his profile already isn't a fit for you, you don't need to dig any deeper. Chances are if you already have concerns, when you learn more, you're going to like less.

Crown Jewel: It is said that opposites attract. While it may be true that we find people with unfamiliar qualities enticing, for longevity in a relationship, shared values and beliefs are of fundamental importance.

Have you put your Ideal Mate List on paper? If you don't have a list, how do you know what you are shopping for? If you don't know the target, how do you know if you've hit it? By now you have been surrounded by plenty of men in your life. What are your personal preferences? Tall, short, dark hair, light hair, no hair, introverted, extroverted, etc. If you don't have your list, create it now. Use all your tricks from your Happy Times List to get yourself into a fun, playful, energetic state and dream up your perfect man. Brainstorm all the characteristics, physical features, interests, hobbies, values, and aspirations of your ideal mate. This is your exceptional dream man—no censoring; absolutely everything you yearn for in a perfect match. Get specific. Get it out of your head and into your heart and onto paper.

You can always change your mind should you so decide. I know—I have on occasion manifested the perfect man only to find, after getting exactly what I had asked for, that it wasn't what I wanted. When I don't care about finances and only want the guy with deep soul, that's exactly what I get, and then I decide I must have someone who is financially secure. Then when I get the guy with total financial security, I decide I need someone more exciting and outside-the-box.

Then when I get the guy who is outrageously exciting and loves to travel the world, I want someone with more stability. What can I say? I'm a woman; I am constantly changing what I want—it's perfectly natural.

I used to think it was me, just my crazy idiosyncrasies, but when I studied more about the innate feminine characteristics women "normally" possess, I learned feminine energy is ever changing. Without a moment's notice, it can go from a full expression of one emotion to a completely different feeling. The beauty of this quality allows women to be attentive to the needs of all those around her, constantly flowing in her energy to best serve herself and her loved ones. This also means that as women, one minute we may love a man, and the next minute he turns our stomach, possibly because of something we are not even conscious of, possibly his tone, his energy. Be aware of your dynamic energy and make certain if you revise your list, it's for good cause. Otherwise maybe you need to revise your viewpoint.

Crown Jewel: It is natural for women to change their minds. It's a very feminine quality.

Really scrutinize what you need versus what you desire. You may even need something you really don't desire in a partner. For example, to be comfortable and have all your needs met, you may need a stable partner, even though you long for that crazy, spontaneous character. I didn't prepare an "I don't want list" or a "must not" list because our unconscious mind does not process the negative words like don't and no. When you say the words "don't" or "no," your unconscious mind goes right past that word to whatever is next and is obligated to deliver. For instance, when I say to myself, "I don't want to eat sugar anymore," all the unconscious recognizes is "eat sugar," and I must obey.

Further, the unconscious acts as an obedient servant and will work to make you right. It will work to make the information you have given it true without regard to whether it is objectively accurate. So if you call yourself a loser, it will work to make you right. But if you call yourself a WINNER, it will work to make you right, and I'd much rather be a winner. If you call yourself a winner, your unconscious will look specifically for your "wins" to reinforce the information provided. Your "wins" can be all accomplishments that lead you in a favorable direction; it doesn't have to be crossing a finish line. With each "win" your unconscious finds, the stronger your belief comes. More on this in Chapter 11.

Crown Jewel: Your unconscious mind doesn't process the negative words like "don't" and "no." Your unconscious will go right past the negative words to whatever is next and deliver it. So, if you don't want to be poor, focus your words on being wealthy. If you don't want to be sad, focus on being happy.

Since my Ideal Mate List is on my phone, it goes everywhere I do. You always hear different theories: review it every day; once you write it, tear it up; speak it out loud; visualize him. I made my list so I could refer to it when I need to determine whether I have hit the target or whether I was even aiming correctly. I do believe flexibility is important. While I would never settle, I would also never be so rigid as to possibly rule out an exceptional man. Occasionally, the traits we are looking for are not overtly displayed. There may be things we need that we aren't aware of until we lack them. As I said, after some dates, I add to the list. Every experience is a learning experience, and I am thankful for the lessons.

The following is my actual Ideal Mate List, taken directly off my phone. I brainstormed all the qualities I could dream of in my perfect match. Anything and everything I could think of to conjure up my Mr. Right. What would I enjoy experiencing with him? What values would we share? What differences would I appreciate? I reflected on prior relationships: What qualities had I appreciated in previous partners? What qualities had they lacked? I got it out of my head and onto paper. The asterisks indicate my "musts."

Ideal Mate List

Respectful

*Spiritual/soulful

*Positive & Loving

Self-development/self-actualized/deep

Charismatic/extroverted/exciting/spontaneous

Out of the box

*Healthy lifestyle-food & exercise/physically fit

*Financially & emotionally secure/freedom/motivated

*Giving/selfless - to me & others

Sweet/affectionate/passionate

*Strong/masculine

*Kissy/touchy/attentive/great lover

Leader/confident

Sweet/soft

Full of life/rhythm

Settled (home/career)

Freedom - has it & encourages it

Appreciates all of me/my core

Adores me as I am/encourages my femininity

*Intelligent/stimulating conversation

Clever/quick witted

*Non-smoker & no drugs

*Monogamous/loyal/devoted/loyal/honest/truthful

Funny/fun/exciting/large personality

Loves travel/new experiences/people

Great dresser/style

Good family/lots friends

Manners/gentleman

Handsome

Great conversationalist/speaks positively

Loves everyone/builds others up/inclusive of others

No desk job/entrepreneurial spirit/diverse

Crown Jewel: He who is the most flexible wins. This is true in all of life—don't get frustrated; get flexible with your time, your energy, your love, and your list. If you learn to roll with the punches, you won't get knocked out.

Pay close attention to what he is looking for as indicated in his profile. Review the standardized questions and his autobiographical portion thoroughly. Though many men will still express interest if you do not precisely meet the search parameters he has listed, it does give you insight into exactly what he's looking for in his ideal partner. Does he want his mate to have a certain level of income? Does he want a partner who has attained a certain educational level? Is he specific in regards to religion or ethnicity? Does he want his woman to look a certain way, i.e., height, body style, hair color, or eye color? Some men have a "type" to which they are repeatedly drawn. As perfect as you are, exactly the way you are, everyone is attracted to some features more than to others. Some are based on physicality and some on personality. There is no right or wrong, only individual preference. Some men wish to date only women who are "geographically correct"—those who live in close proximity—so check to see if you are within the mileage area he has listed.

Crown Jewel: Review the qualities he has indicated he is searching for in a partner. While most men are not hard and fast on these preferences, it will give you insight into what he is looking for.

I know it's a sore subject, but age can also be of importance. Men can have children up to a much greater age than women, so often, older men are looking for younger women of childbearing age. Sometimes, however, it's another screening mechanism for looks and vibrancy. You can look at his preference for wanting kids to better assess his intent. I know it is quite common for both men and women to lie about their age online. I also know you can have a very young fifty-year-old or a very old fifty-year-old. If you pay attention to all the details in his profile, messages, and phone conversations, you can get a fairly good indication of his age and vitality before ever meeting him in person. In most cases, a man will have multiple pictures posted. Make certain to look at all the pictures. Often, younger versions are mixed in with older.

If you decide you would like to search online yourself for possible candidates, feel free to do so, even send an *indication of interest,* but don't become the aggressor. You want an exceptional man, and an exceptional man needs to be the pursuer. You are worth it. It's nature at its best. Similarly to other social media sites, many online dating sites provide a feature that permits a member to review a list of every user who has visited his or her profile. This option allows you to see who has been checking out your profile regardless of whether they have contacted you. I promise men online are perpetually looking. They are efficiently checking every possible resource, including this feature. Feel free to look at all the profiles and photos as you wish. He's smart; he'll know you've been there, and if he's interested, he'll *indicate interest*—or better yet, message you.

Crown Jewel: You don't have to initiate contact. He'll know you've looked at his profile. All men online know about the feature that allows them to review who's been looking at their profile, and they All use this option regularly. If he's interested, he'll contact you.

Rarely, a man will hide his profile, so you cannot see that he has visited your profile. Most dating sites have an option to allow you to temporarily hide your profile without having to close your account. If you hide your profile, this will normally permit you to search online without the men knowing you have viewed their profiles. However, be aware that the site may have logged your visit, so when you unhide your profile, it then shows that you have previously viewed his profile. This feature to hide your profile will allow you to take breaks periodically, such as when you find a possible exceptional man you wish to date exclusively. If you take a dating hiatus, you can return by simply reactivating or unhiding your profile rather than starting a new profile from scratch. Normally, you can use this option by clicking one button to take your profile offline or to hide it, and then just one click again to reactive your profile—assuming any subscription fees are current. Taking your profile offline doesn't normally suspend your subscription or fees.

Some sites have an option to create a search in which matches will be emailed to you on a regular basis. Spend the time on this one to be specific and answer every question. Study the Ideal Mate List you have created. Focus on your "must haves" and if you have any, your "must not haves." I decided physical appearance was less crucial than depth and security. I ruled out only those categories absolutely intolerable to me. It's different for everyone. It may be politics or religion. It may be hair or exercise, or lack thereof. You want to keep your pool of potential exceptional men as large as possible. You can always, always modify your search if you discover an additional "must" or "must not." Once you have created a search of men explicitly customized to the qualities you are looking for in a partner, you can have the list emailed to you regularly. Now that you have a pool of suitors and you have chosen those you would like to learn more about, you can dive into the next level of online interaction.

Crown Jewel: Some dating sites reveal when you are online. Check to see if you can turn this feature OFF or be aware it will indicate your status to everyone.

Chapter Eight:

How to Connect with Potential Matches

Have confidence and know your exceptional man will gravitate toward that confidence you exude. You don't have to chase after him; he will come to you. Throughout the ages, women have realized that men respond to challenges. Why do you think men love sports? Men love contests, and you are the ultimate prize. The harder they have to work to get your attention, the more they relish that attention. You teach people how to treat you. If you command respect, you will receive it. If you love yourself, others can't help but love you. Let a man pursue you; it will make you both feel better. It's how they're built. I know this myself from my Groundhog Day approach. I tried to randomly talk to guys I was attracted to at bars, I texted, I called—it never worked. It's too aggressive. When a gentleman does approach you, don't talk about how marriage-minded you are or how you can't wait to have kids. Don't get desperate; he's on his way. Use the time in preparation of his arrival.

Once a man has initiated contact and you have determined yourself to be interested, you should wait a bit to respond. You don't want to spend all your time online, and you never want to appear overly eager or anxious. You are a busy woman with an amazingly full life. If the man only *indicates interest*, simply respond with an *indication of interest*, not a message. Frequently a guy will *indicate interest* and then determine he should have put forth more effort, so he will follow up with a message. If he has messaged you, then respond with a message in kind. When corresponding, always, always use positive vocabulary. Let me reiterate: you always want to start and finish every conversation, whether virtual or otherwise, on a positive note, even if a negative is in the middle. I've heard this referred to as the positive sandwich effect. In a message it would go something like this: "I think you are a lovely man, though I don't think we're a match. I wish you the best of luck in your search."

Crown Jewel: Positive sandwich: You always want to start and finish a conversation on a positive note, even if there is a negative statement in the middle. Review the positive language list in Chapter 4.

Begin your message with a well-wishing of some sort. For example, "I hope you are having a super Sunday funday," or "I hope you are enjoying this beautiful weather," and end with the more of the same: "Wishing you a wonderful week" or "Hope you have the best day ever." If you are attempting to get closer, you might use, "Looking forward to speaking" or "Looking forward to learning more." On salutations, I always use "Smiles, Drea." Since my user name is "SmilesSassClass," I think it's a playful tie-in. However, if I have not progressed to a point at which I feel comfortable revealing my name, I simply write just, "Smiles." You can always use a salutation and then your user name. For instance, I could use "Smiles, SmilesSassClass." You can see why this doesn't work, but if your user name were "MissBliss," it would be "Smiles, MissBliss." How cute is that? It takes only a few extra seconds to add these touches, but can make him feel so warm and cared for. If you don't believe me, try it on your girlfriends or colleagues.

Crown Jewel: In life, you get back the energy you put out. Put positive energy into that message, that phone conversation, or that date.

When you send each email this week at work, to friends, or to family, add positive energy with one of these lines and check out the response you get. It will make every interaction more pleasant. Your positive energy will set the tone of any exchange to follow. People will respond with more enthusiasm. They will want to help you more with whatever you need. You also always take an extra moment to create a tagline for the "Re" section of the email as well. I frequently use "Smile & the world smiles with you." Since my user name is SmilesSassClass, it's a catchy and cheerful way to convey how I think and feel. Attention to detail can draw your exceptional man in, and you are an exceptional woman who deserves nothing less.

If you're reviewing your inbox very late at night or very early in the morning, draft an email but do not send it until the timing is right. You can simply save the email as a draft if the dating site offers that option. This tool can be handy even during the day. I will prepare an email and save it as a draft until a sufficient time has passed or the time of day is right so that I am ready to send it. As I mentioned, men need to feel they are the pursuer. If you crave immediate attention, go love on your pet or pull out your Happy Times List. Some dating sites sell an additional notification package that allows members to purchase a special alert that informs that member you have opened a message from him. You should be aware that if he has this feature, he is notified immediately when you read his message.

Crown Jewel: Most online dating sites provide cell phone applications.

In online dating, and messaging in general, people tend to use the same vernacular over and over. I'm often messaged or see the same lines verbatim in profiles. As we know, people are engaging in such a large number of interactions online that they have developed quick systems of inquiries and answers. I have also developed responses utilizing my Groundhog Day approach to common inquires and messages I receive. You never want to have a generic, humdrum response. The following are some examples of the common statements I see from men online and some of my responses.

He said:

Apparently, these are some of his favorite lines:

I think we have a lot in common.

Call me or text 867-5309. (Tommy Tutone's "Jenny" 1982)

Will you marry me? LOL

Hi:) How r u?

How's this site treating you?

I don't come on here often, call me at 867-5309.

I don't like to waste time messaging all the time.

Let's meet for coffee?

You look familiar.

I am new to this...

I'm not sure why I'm doing this.

I know I'm not in your age range but...

According to this site, we're a good fit.

I would like to get to know you.

You are beautiful.

Wink

Let's chat.

I tried this because I work all the time.

You caught my eye.

My membership expires tomorrow.

If you're interested hit me up.

How long have you been on here?

Do you ever make it to _X_ city (the city where he lives)?

Your profile was a pleasant surprise.

How was your weekend?

I know I don't live near you, but...

Do you have an Instagram/Facebook?

I noticed you viewed my profile...

What do you do for work?

I never thought I would be online dating.

How long have you been on here?

I'm over the club scene.

My friends say I'm a nice/great guy.

She said:

These are some of my favorite lines:

Good morning, good afternoon, good evening

Smile & the world smiles with you.

I would welcome the opportunity to learn more.

Heart of the South

Coffee, tea or...

Ready to travel no baggage.

Yes sir, I would love to...

he, he, he...

I'm rather traditional...feel free to call me at 867-5309.

I would welcome the opportunity to speak with you...

Sounds lovely...

I'm fantastic.. How are you?

Hope you are having a wonderful week.

You got Mail:)

Wishing you the best day ever.

Crown Jewel: "My membership expires tomorrow, call me at 867-5309." If they use this line, you can simply respond with a message. If they're really interested, they will pay the price—literally.

Men and women commonly use text acronyms in messages and emails. Acronyms are abbreviations for words or groups of words formed from the initial letters of the original words. I never take the shortcut in emails. I am fully invested in the process and take the time to respond to only those men who have piqued my curiosity, so when I do respond, I give them my full attention. In this case, attention to detail can make all the difference. You want to be aware that there can easily be interpretation issues in the written word, so be particularly mindful when texting, direct messaging, or emailing. You don't want him to misconstrue the message you are trying to convey. When emailing, space is usually unlimited; however, in text messaging, these acronyms come in very handy, as the number of characters permitted is limited. See the complete Text Acronym Dictionary at the end of the book.

Examples of common text acronyms:

DM	Direct message
LOL	laugh out loud
LMAO	laughing my a** off
TTYL	talk to you later
BFF	best friend forever
QT	cutie
GR8	great
XOXO	hugs and kisses
R	are
U	you
UR	your

The following are common text visuals:

(These are all viewed sideways)

:) or :-)	means happy
:(or :-(	means sad
;) or ;-)	means winking happy
<3	means heart

If a guy contacts you with something like "Hi," and after reviewing his profile you determine you would like to take your online conversation deeper, you might try revealing something about yourself, possibly even something already listed in your profile, and then stating, "I would welcome the opportunity to learn more..." Profiles may be vague, and you want to learn as much as possible so as to better prescreen eligible men. Don't reveal anything so personal that you could be located or possibly put yourself in danger. Sometimes an online man will ask for personal information such as my Instagram, Facebook, or my direct email address, which I never release. He can get to know you through messaging on the dating site or phone calls if you have progressed to that point.

Crown Jewel: If a man asks for my Instagram/Facebook account information, I simply explain that I use my account professionally as well as personally and do not release that information.

You do not need to respond to unsolicited messages and certainly not to an *indication of interest* if you do not wish to pursue the communication. If you choose you may use a "No, thank you" option, if available, which automates that reply. If you message a man you are not interested in to thank him for his compliments, it leads him to believe he may have a chance. Occasionally, after reviewing a profile, I may find the man is exceptional, just not an ideal match for me. I will send him a message letting him know that while I think he is fantastic, "I don't think we're a match, but I have a girlfriend I think might be." Every gentleman I have ever approached with this has been completely receptive. I will connect the two and then let nature do its work.

If you are interested in a gentleman who has messaged you, answer his questions in a cute, flirtatious manner and then follow-up with a return question to him. You want to give him a reason to respond to your message. Let him get a feel for how fun it's going to be with you in person. Keep your messages brief. Pick something personal out of his profile and write a positive comment on it. For example, if he has written about his vacation snow skiing, you might write, "Skiing is so exciting; I love the snow," or if he recently jumped out of a plane, "I can't believe you have been skydiving; you are very courageous." Take the extra time to make it personal and really connect. This could be your exceptional mate. Isn't he worth it?

Crown Jewel: Keep your messages brief. If you're interested, you want to progress quickly to the phone, then a live date, in order to determine the real chemistry.

If you want another message from him, make certain you ask him a question he needs to respond to. You might personalize it by asking questions regarding things you find interesting in his profile. It's less imposing if you give the information you are requesting. For example, I use the conversation starter, "I'm from Charleston. Where are you from originally?" This puts him more at ease, and it feels like a reciprocal gesture to answer the question. You might try something like, "I was a runner in college and love the outdoors. I enjoy running along the beach every morning. What do you enjoy for exercise?" Who, what, when, and where are all closed questions to gather information. Why and how are open questions to generate discussion. I have found you must be very tactful in asking about a man's work. Often, they feel they are being qualified. No one wants to feel judged. You may instead ask about his passions and mission. Often his profile discloses what he does for a living.

Don't be scared to let him know you're interested. I'm certain you're well aware that you don't have to be live and in front of someone to flirt. Emails, texts, and phone conversations all afford the opportunity as well. Flirting is a playful way of communicating with a man to show him your interest without verbally telling him. Not only will it show him you're interested but also it can be fun for you both. People like it when you speak in their language. I take note of phrases he repeatedly uses or how he asks the questions and respond with the same.

For example, if he tells me he "love[s] to experience live sporting events," I might respond with, "I love to experience life as well; I recently visited Hawaii. Where was your last vacation?" It's Groundhog Day again if you try questions or comments and get a less than favorable response on the next guy, try a different tactic.

Crown Jewel: People like it when you speak in their language. I make note of phrases he repeatedly uses or how he asks the questions and respond with the same verbiage.

Every now and again, a guy without a primary profile picture or additional photos will write indicating he would like to email or text photos directly to me. If he hasn't posted a picture and blames his career, clients, or his high-profile status, he's generally just embarrassed, although I have heard of married men using this trick. After reviewing a profile and determining I am interested, I welcome the member to send me photos. On occasion, he will request my personal email, which I will never give him. You can usually message photos directly through the dating site. If he can't figure it out, I copy and paste the instructions, which are typically found under the site's help section, and message those instructions directly to him through the site. To copy the instructions on a Mac/Apple computer, highlight them, then hold the *command* key and press the letter *C* key; to paste, go to your message where you want the text to appear and hold the *command* key and press the letter *V* key. On Windows it is exactly the same, but the command key is replaced with the *control* key. Some men don't have a primary photo posted, but if you open their profile, you are able to see the additional photos.

One of my pet peeves online is when a guy initiates contact, then requests you to come to his area of town. I don't mind the driving aspect one bit, but it's setting the tone for any relationship to follow. You teach people how to treat you, and I don't care if he looks like Brad Pitt and has the finances of Warren Buffett, I'm a lady and deserve to be treated as such. I respond, "I'm rather traditional. I don't feel appropriate traveling to a man on a first date." After getting to know me, a gentleman better understands my Southern roots, and he doesn't even ask me to come to his location on future dates—instead he will often offer to pick me up. Most men are very receptive and respect that I am a lady, and if not, well, he's not my exceptional man, anyway, so I am able to conserve my energy for that man who might be

Crown Jewel: You teach people how to treat you, and I don't care if he looks like Brad Pitt and has the finances of Warren Buffet. YOU are a LADY and deserve to be treated as such.

If he is that man who might be my exceptional man, well, I want to speak to that man. Speaking on the phone brings an entirely new element into the interaction. It's so exciting to feel his energy through the phone. You will now not only get to find out in greater detail who he is, but you will learn even more through the inflections in his voice. You can determine how confidently he speaks, the certainty in his tone, and how positive his energy is. There is so much more that is revealed in a person's speech than in the written word. In writing, there is time for contemplation and deliberate word selection. The written word is fixed, while the spoken word is flowing. When one articulates any thought, the words include not only the pronunciation, but also a certain tone or pitch, speed, and volume. There is often even great meaning in any pauses. Think about reading a book versus listening to the audio or viewing the movie. Oftentimes people think a movie is terrible when it comes from a book they have read and loved because in their mind's eye, with the words provided in the book they created their own images perfectly suited to their ideals. No director could match each person's visions so perfectly.

Crown Jewel: I generally respond to only two or three messages, then direct the contact to a phone conversation.

Getting to the Phone

If you have determined this man is someone you would like to take the conversation to the next level with, simply write "I would love to catch up via phone...867-5309," or possibly "I would love to hear the sound of your voice...867-5309." Men relentlessly give me their numbers, requesting I phone or text them. I will never call or text a man first. Every move you make will set the tone for a relationship that could follow. My exceptional man will be unambiguously that: a man. I respond with, "I would welcome the opportunity to learn more about you. I'm rather traditional...867-5309." In my experience, men love this. I am rather traditional and extremely feminine, so if he's not comfortable making the moves, it's indicative of a mismatch.

Once you have given him your number, put it out of your mind. Some men online don't follow up, but many do. Sometimes it takes an online gentleman as much as several weeks to call you once he receives your number. Just like men you meet offline, those you meet online may be preoccupied with other activities, i.e. work, school, travel, children, etc. Trust in fate and enjoy the process. Don't make up a fantasy in your head thinking he is the most perfect man you will ever come across. Don't start planning the wedding and naming the children. Your exceptional man will be there when the time is right.

Crown Jewel: It may take a gentleman, whether you meet him online or offline, as much as several weeks to actually call you once he receives your number.

I always, always let numbers I can't identify go straight to voice mail. It could be business, or it could be pleasure calling. I want to be mentally prepared to speak with whoever is on the line. If you are fully present in each moment, you won't be constantly watching your phone. You won't be preoccupied in anticipation of a text, call, or email. Be fully invested in whatever opportunity is currently before you. You never want to be so anxious that you pick up every single phone call you receive. You want to be fully prepared and completely present for your conversation with him, so you must know it's him calling. You have a wonderful life and are full from the inside out. Your exceptional man will be an added enhancement in your already exceptional life. I usually wait a day or so before I ring him back. I'm a busy woman and fit him in when I can, but he is not a priority—yet.

Another reason to answer only when you can identify it's your potential exceptional man calling is the voice in which you answer. When I was running my law firm, my friends who phoned me at work would tease me for my "work voice." Isn't this true with us all? When our mom calls, we have one voice. When our boss calls us, we have another. When our best friend calls, yet another. You want to take his call when you have the time to really focus on him. You want to put your most attractive voice forward when your exceptional man calls. Make certain you know whom you are answering the phone for so you can put forth the energy you choose.

I swear, the harder a man has to work for the prize, the more he cherishes it. As I said, men respond to challenges, they love the thrill of the chase, and you are the ultimate prize. Men like it when they feel you are not needy but are actually making time for them. If you are eagerly awaiting his every response, he will sense your neediness. I notice that the more a gentleman has to work for a date with me, the more effort he puts into that date. He puts more thought and energy into arranging the logistics and allocates more time with me for the date. He has so much invested that he wants to give it his all to make the date a success. Instead of coffee, it becomes dinner or the theater.

After determining from his voice mail that a suitor is calling, I program in his number with PC (Prince Charming) before his name, identifying to only me that he is an online gentleman caller. Then I take a photo with my phone of his profile picture so that not only do I know what my suitor looks like, but I have already internally and unconsciously stored my feeling of him connected to that photo. I pick my favorite photo from his profile since I know that every time I see that picture, I will be more attracted, whereas if I choose a less attractive photo, it would have the opposite effect, and I might find myself less attracted to him before I've even met him in person. A picture speaks a thousand words, and I want all of mine to be positive on my prospective Prince Charming.

Crown Jewel: I take a photo with my phone of his best profile picture and store it with his phone number under PC, then his name to identify to only me he is an online gentleman caller.

Rarely, a guy will call and not leave a message. This guy is not your exceptional man. You are a busy, exceptional woman, and your exceptional man will not expect you to take every call. Don't make up an excuse about how he wants you to answer the phone so he can speak directly with you, or maybe your voice mail didn't pick up. Never call a number back to see if it's him calling you. Your mental preparedness will allow you to harness your exceptional energy. Your finesse will jump right through that phone and capture his attention. He'll be dying to meet you in person. If I return a call and the gentleman doesn't answer, I always leave a message. Don't wait and call back again later; this looks desperate.

Just like every other interaction you have, you want to be positive, positive, positive when you talk on the phone. Keep all your conversations light and fun. I am constantly giggling in conversations with a man. I love to learn about him, and there is always something that tickles me about what he has to say. You want to give him a taste of how pleasurable it's going to be when you meet in person. You have already prescreened him based on his entire profile and messages exchanged. While you may use the phone conversation to further screen, you don't want to make that your expectation or it will feel that way to him. Allow your purpose in speaking to emanate your radiance through the phone and establish a time and location for your date.

Crown Jewel: Always end the conversation first, leaving him wanting more.

When deciding on when and where to meet in person, remember: SAFETY FIRST. Yes, you know it—buckle up and enjoy the ride; make certain you are well protected. Always agree to meet in a public place with lots of people around. I generally follow his lead and allow him to arrange the date as long as it is within these safety boundaries. As I indicated earlier, I always have a gentleman come to my area of town for a first date. I'm a lady, and even in this nontraditional dating experience, I expect the man to be a gentleman. I enjoy a man considering my needs and putting forth the effort to schedule the date. Typically, a gentleman will ask what I like and then plan accordingly. To me it is indicative of his attention and the quality of any relations to follow.

I always send one of my girlfriends my date's contact information and his user name. If it's a third or fourth date and I agree to ride with him, I advise him I have forwarded his information to a friend. I believe a gentleman should pick you up at the door, but not on the first date, and always, safety first. Never, ever get drunk or do anything else that could impair your judgment. You want to make an exceptional impression, and nobody thinks the cute drunk girl at the bar is all that cute. You want to keep your personal items in your visual proximity at all times; you don't want to risk any private information getting stolen or your drink being spiked by anyone. The exceptional man you are looking for will most certainly understand you are an intelligent woman who will protect her own safety, even though your gut is assuring you that he is a perfect gentleman. You're a super smart, exceptional woman who knows how to protect herself while at the same time enjoying herself on a date. You are always prepared for whatever may come.

Speaking on the phone is an exciting way to get a little test of how that chemistry's going to be. It gives you a teaser with the inflection in his voice and his choice of words. You can see how he responds, the speed and tone of his speech, where he pauses, how his thoughts flow. You've got even more information now to be fully prepared to meet him live and in person. Now that you've determined he is a potentially exceptional man, it really gets fun—you get to meet him up close and personal. He gets the opportunity to see what an exceptional woman you are and enjoy your presence, and in return you get the same.

Dating can be so much fun, particularly when you've already prescreened your date. Irrespective of the chemistry, you know you've picked a great guy, so you're going to have a great time.

Chapter Nine:

Preparing to Meet Your Date in Person

The practice round prepares you for the real game. Preparation, as with any skill set you want to fully develop, is key. Just as in preparing for your photos, you want to be fully equipped for your face-to-face encounter. Exercise all that confidence you have developed throughout your entire life. First impressions are everything, and since this is your first time meeting live and in person, it's still a first impression. You never get a second chance to make a first impression. He's never been up close and personal with you, and he could be your exceptional man. Take the time to get all gussied up for him. Olfactory, which is smell, is your strongest sense, and you're going to be in close proximity, so make certain you have fresh breath. A hint of perfume, not overdone, is a nice touch as well.

You will feel your best when you make the extra effort to look your best. Dress appropriately for the date location and time of day. You are a brilliant, gorgeous, exceptional woman—let it show in every detail. When preparing for your date, don't just take care of what's on the outside, take care of what's most important: what's going on inside. Show your attention to detail, externally and internally—let him see your beauty.

Crown Jewel: In prepping your feminine energy for a date, dance to bring forth all your radiance. Just turn on your music at home, by yourself, and let it flow from your body. Your glow will be irresistible. Review your Feminine Times List created in Chapter 4 and play with your favorites.

In looking for your exceptional man, you must be that exceptional woman he seeks. You must become that which you wish to attract. What qualities is he looking for? What do you need to expand in your life, or clean out, to make room for him? You don't get what you want—you get what you are. Like attracts like. Do you have some bad habits you want to change, maybe some patterns you'd like to interrupt? Ninety-five percent of our thoughts are the same thoughts as the day before. You become what you think about. What dominates your thought patterns? Spend the time and do the work on yourself so you will be that you wish to attract. You are a perfect being; just bring forth all that's already inside you. Embody all that you seek. Polish those diamonds you love about yourself so they shine brightly. Let the light in and the love out. You are a priceless jewel. Treasure yourself.

Crown Jewel: Thought is energy. The energy of your thoughts draws to you matching vibrational energies. Whether it be people or things, like attracts like.

If you know he's not the one and you're only going out to entertain yourself, it is better to save your energy for when that exceptional man does show up. Albert Einstein is acclaimed as one of the greatest thinkers ever to have walked the earth. He intentionally did not memorize his own telephone number, feeling it was an inadequate use of valuable life energy. We choose what information we designate as minutia. Leave the unimportant at the curb to save room for what really matters. Use your precious life energy to go out with your girlfriends or to work on becoming the woman who would attract the kind of exceptional man you crave. Take the time to read a good, uplifting book, get some exercise, or meditate on finding your exceptional man. Go back to your Happy Times List and follow through on some of those activities. When you keep having unfavorable dating experiences because you don't prescreen properly, it may deter you from continuing your journey to your exceptional man.

Don't get discouraged because you go out with every guy who initiates contact with you. You are spectacular; of course, he wants to share your company, but you get to be the judge.

As with any interview, you always want to be on time. Some people feel a sense of disrespect when an appointment shows up late. I don't like to be late ever, and used to hate it when others were late to meet me. I felt it was selfish and a sign of disrespect. You know what? All that did was frustrate me and make it an awkward, unpleasant event when the person did finally arrive. You are happy in direct proportion to the amount of control you feel you have over your life. I accept full responsibility for everything that occurs in my life. I have put myself in every place, at every moment. I control everything. Now I choose: I can either wait on someone because I really want to see this person, or I can leave. I am always in control of the situation, and how I react is my decision. I make certain I'm always on time, then I choose if he's worth waiting for. For a first encounter, you never want to be late. But there's a catch: you don't want to be early, either.

It's a little tricky with a blind date. You don't want to appear overly eager and be early, but you definitely don't want to appear rude and be late. If I arrive to the date destination early, I sit in my car somewhere nearby so as not to go in before the scheduled time. If he phones or texts saying he is delayed, I delay my entry. When looking for your blind date, if he is not already awaiting you at the door, remember you have his picture on your phone to reference. I look at this photo before exiting my car so as to not be fidgeting with my phone should he be awaiting my arrival. After we locate each other, I put my phone in my purse, on vibrate, the entire date. I have my phone with me to be safe, but never pay it any attention whatsoever. No sneaking it out in the bathroom for a quickie text.

When you finally meet him in person, the same philosophy applies as when messaging and conversing on the phone: positive, positive, positive. You never want to criticize or complain about anyone or anything. A person's name is the sweetest sound on earth to that person, so be certain you have the pronunciation correct and use it often, but not so much as to look as if you are trying too hard. Be conscious of interrupting your date or dominating the conversation. You are here to learn about him. Listen to what he has to say and follow up with questions that demonstrate you are interested. People can think much quicker than they can speak, so listening gives you plenty of time to anticipate your next question. If you recall, who, what, when, and where are all closed questions to gather information. Why and how are open questions to generate discussion. You are an intelligent, deep woman, and you have all the tools of the most powerful communicators on earth. You now get to use all those tools you've learned. You want to make a perfect first impression, and you will because you are exceptional.

Crown Jewel: A person's name is the sweetest sound on earth to that person, so be certain you have the pronunciation correct and use it intermittently. Listen to learn. Listen to understand. Listen to be a great communicator.

All this doesn't mean don't be real. Be real, but accentuate the positive and eliminate the negative. You are exceptional exactly as you are; let him see your incredible true nature. Show sincere gratitude for all of the blessings in your life. Everything you have ever done has gotten you to this amazing point of existence. Honestly express appreciation for yourself and your world for the unbelievable woman you are. The more you adore yourself, the more others will be drawn to adore you. They can't help it; it's magnetic. With the heightened popularity of online dating, there are such vast numbers of potential partners that a guy will already be thinking of his next match if you don't capture his attention immediately. Don't be scared, promptly upon meeting him, if you know you're interested. Radiate your magnificent energy. This doesn't mean be forward or overtly sexual; just expressively divulge the chemistry you feel. It will be an enchanting evening for you both. Let the sparks fly.

Crown Jewel: Confidence is key. Tips to show your self-confidence: Look your best, but be comfortable in your skin with whatever look you choose, and don't fidget. You can use conversation starters in Chapter 12, listen carefully, and maintain direct eye contact as discussed in Chapter 11.

Flirt with him. Show, don't tell, him you are interested. Now is the time to use all those nonverbal subtleties you are learning. Send out energy with every micro-movement of your body. Flash a coy smile, make eye contact, and mirror his body language. To create more intimacy, you may lean in closer to him to show your interest in what he's saying or lower your voice intentionally so he has to lean closer to hear you. As women, we make preening moves that exhibit interest in men, like twirling our hair, putting on lipstick, and straightening our clothes. You may touch or subtly stroke part of your body, or you may even gently touch him. We use these nonverbal cues, both consciously and unconsciously, to draw awareness to our feminine features. We may call his attention to our lips by touching them, putting on lipstick, or licking them. This can encourage men to anticipate kissing them. Most women are not aware that spreading their fingers and making soft movements in the hips and shoulders, like a sway, invite a man's attention as well. Move that gorgeous body— play with these tools.

Crown Jewel: If a gentleman is teasing you or slightly challenging you in a playful way, he's flirting with you. My Granny used to always say, if he pulls your hair, he likes you.

If you have a hard time connecting, get straight to the heart of things. Look into his eyes, even if you know he is not your exceptional man. Give him this gift, and give yourself this gift as well. I really mean look. Focus both of your eyes into his left eye, and don't look away for at least twenty seconds. It's okay to blink, but hold total eye contact, expressing your love for him as a human being. This will connect the two of you on a deeper level. Don't be scared; give him your undivided attention. Most people look at other people all day long without really seeing them. They have conversations in which they look straight at each other and speak without even really making any connection at all. I found that I often focus on people's lips when conversing in order to better interpret what they are saying, but by doing so there is a disconnect on the intimacy side of the conversation. It's more babble than an interpersonal connection. If you're really in sync with this man, don't just have a pleasant conversation—connect with him on a deep, energetic level. Resonate with his vibrational level and feel the energy he needs from you—no holding back.

Rapport-building Techniques

If you really feel him and really believe he could be your exceptional man, allow your breath to mirror his. To mirror means to make the same movements he is making at the same time he is making them, as if you were looking into a mirror. While looking into his eyes, in your peripheral vision notice his breath pattern. You can see his shoulders or chest rise when he inhales; follow that breath with yours. Literally breathe in and out at the same time as he does. This will connect you two even deeper. When you mirror someone, you take on the same physiology, the same postures and positions he is in. This makes people more connected to you, thus more comfortable with you. Notice that this also makes you more comfortable with him. If you want him to feel you more—emotionally, not physically—then mirror him. Practice with your girlfriends first; learn how to connect deeply without uttering a word. Enjoy the depth of connection you can experience with this one simple technique.

Crown Jewel: Unless your date is chewing gum and you are using it as a rapport tactic, I would advise against chewing gum; most people don't see it as incredibly sexy.

When mirroring someone, first synchronize breathing, then tune in to his volume, speed, tonality, and words. You can copy his arm movements, stance, and facial expressions. All this leads to building rapport. Everyone knows how to achieve rapport with others; we do it every day. Rapport is a term used to describe the feeling of being in sync with each other—on the same wavelength. The main ways to build rapport are mirroring and matching body language, breath, and eye contact.

Mirroring and matching both involve body language, which encompasses gestures, breathing speed and location, and voice tone, speed, and volume. The only difference in mirroring and matching is which side of the body you use. In mirroring you use the opposite side of the body when facing the individual; you are, in effect, becoming his mirror image; whereas in matching you use the same side of the body as the person you are facing. I personally find mirroring a bit more connecting.

Crown Jewel: When we speak to the bank teller, when the bag boy helps us with our groceries, or when we ask for the time from a stranger, these acts bring us in rapport. It's all about the connection with the people we're asking, not simply about getting what we need from them.

The biggest key in rapport is flexibility. You must be able to follow his body language and breathe, wherever it takes you. He may breathe fast or slow; or he may breathe deep or shallow. You follow wherever he leads. It is said that he who is the most flexible wins. I believe this is true in life and definitely makes the adventure much more pleasurable. Think about all that undue stress produced by your wanting to have everything perfect. Have fewer constraints on your ideals about exactly how life has to be and exactly how people have to behave. Most stress comes from blowing issues out of proportion. In the spectrum of life, what does it really matter? Put everything in context. Check to make certain your ideals aren't in conflict with one another. For example, if you want a man who can travel the world with you on a moment's notice, yet at the same time you want a man with stability and a family, these may not be traits that can coexist in one individual. Men and women differ in the qualities they find most significant in a partner. Understanding how men think will help you better understand what they are looking for in their ideal mate.

Chapter Ten:

Understanding and Appreciating Our Differences

Masculine men don't really need to hear all about your job or your qualifications. I found men were less than enthusiastic that I was an accomplished attorney who had done X, Y, and Z; but when I told them I loved to dance and pink was my favorite color, you should see the response. A man isn't looking to date another man. He's looking for a woman. Your career is part of what makes you the exceptional woman you are, but when engaging a man, it's about how you make him feel, and to make him feel his best, you must feel yours. Spend the energy on yourself and then spend the energy on him. The level of energy you put out is the level of energy you get back. It's vibrational—like a tuning fork.

Try this simple exercise: the next time you say "hello" to a person on the street or engage with the clerk at a cash register, speak with a *confident enthusiasm* and watch that person's response. After that, on your next interaction, practice your "hello," utilizing your *feminine goddess power*. Then on the following person, try saying "hello" with your *sweet little girl energy*. Try it on both men and women and witness the different response to each energy you put out.

You will see that in every moment, your distinctive flavor or mood can affect the energy you put out, which affects the energy you get back. I love to witness feminine women in their divine beauty. Men also love to be in the presence of and share energy with feminine women. Don't tame the exceptional feminine goddess that you are, unleash her.

Crown Jewel: Men will be impressed with the strength in your femininity. Masculine men aren't looking to date masculine women.

The beautiful thing about intimate relationships is the polarity of men and women. Sexual attraction stems from that polarity. Our differences complement one another; they are reciprocal energies. Women want to be cherished and adored, while men want to be respected and appreciated. Femininity flows while masculinity provides a safe structure for that movement.

Feminine energy responds to praise, it dies without attention, it is the delicate life force, its energy is constantly changing and loves movement, it is free-flowing and non-directional, it always remembers, and it makes little things bigger. I've realized, as a woman, that we never really want space; when I run, I want my man to chase me. When I pull away, I want him to hold me tightly. Feminine energy loves to fill up everything; it fills space with knickknacks, and it fills internally with connection.

I absolutely love to witness men being men. Men want to take care of and protect their women. Masculine energy responds to challenge, it is directional, it is linear in thinking, and purposefully driven. It makes things smaller and wants to bring things to an end; it is rational and structured; it needs appreciation and respect. It seeks to dominate, commonly forgets, and craves freedom. Masculine energy doesn't finesse, it's not delicate and gentle, it's forceful and strong. When men become aware of your needs, they attempt to take care of them. All men do this; it's how they are built.

All men and women have masculine and feminine energies within them. We aren't exclusive to just one, but as women we naturally gravitate toward our true core feminine essence. The more feminine you become, the more aware you will become of these inherent differences. The more you embrace your femininity, the more masculine a man will become in your presence. Again, it's that polarity or reciprocal energies at work. I lived for many years in my masculine shell as an attorney. You need those skills to excel in the business world, but I have realized that to excel in the dating world, you need to embrace your femininity. I am attracted to masculine men, and masculine men are attracted to feminine women. When I started practicing how to get back to my true core feminine energy, I loved it. I started dancing again, I softened, and I started feeling more. It's truly who I am; I had just been putting on that masculine armor to protect myself and succeed "in a man's world."

Crown Jewel: Men love it when you display your femininity openly. Wear a dress, paint your nails, even wear a flower in your hair—men will find your essence irresistible.

I recently noticed this distinct difference when I had a girlfriend come visit me for ten days. She had never been to Charleston and wanted to try everything and go everywhere. She was a very feminine woman and flowed all over the place. I had to figure out all the things she was interested in, schedule the calendar, and figure out the logistics. I had to continuously count her down on time each time we were going anywhere, and it was all exhausting. As soon as she left, I went on a date and became aware of how much I enjoyed a man arranging the destination, the time of departure, all the logistics, even his picking out the food after determining I like fish and veggies. I don't even care if he takes the long way to get there anymore, as long as I don't have to think about it. He considered my needs and took care of everything without a second thought. I love men being men.

Men are wonderful creatures seeking to serve women and make them happy, but no two men are alike. Each one is a spectacular, one-of-a-kind creation. How fortunate that no two women are looking for exactly the same qualities in a partner. You are the Judge. That being said, don't be too quick to judge. In life, there are no absolutes. We are all humans seeing the world from our individual perspective. Men and women process information very differently. People say one "sees the world through rose-colored glasses" when that person thinks everything goes his or her way. Well, you know pink's my favorite color. At least one of two things can always happen; always look for the one you want. I chose to postulate the world as a wonderful place in which I am intended to have fun. I am a favored child of God—and so are you. No matter what people think of me, I always believe they love me and are on my side—and why won't they be? We are all here to share in this experience and connect. I know the same is true for you because you are an exceptional woman. I love you already.

Men see the world through their own set of glasses. Instinctively men are always looking to find out what the point of the conversation is. Men always want to solve the problem. If you express a problem to a man, he assumes you are seeking his expertise in that area and that you are asking for his advice. He doesn't realize you may wish to emote without seeking any answers. Just as when you run out of a room swearing you never want to see him again, he doesn't realize you really want him to chase you and swear he will never let you go.

We aren't trained in how men think, nor are men trained how women think. We are taught that we are all the same. We are schooled that boys and girls are equal, but I have no desire to be a man. I love and embrace the differences. Men and women are perfect reciprocal energies. What one needs the other provides; it's inherent in nature. Treat a man as if he is your hero, and he'll show up as your hero. Rarely do individuals respond to negative reinforcement, but they do respond to positive reinforcement.

Crown Jewel: Men and women are very different. Men are always attempting to problem-solve or get to the point in a conversation, while often women just want the opportunity to express their emotions and be comforted.

In reality, the only reality is the way we decipher it based on every experience we have ever had. For example, I have a friend who is color-blind. She sees only in black or white and shades of gray. If I insist something is red, is it red to her, or is it still black and white? Is she wrong because she can't see it red? We can see only based on our vision. Our vision is tied to our brain and experiences in the world. Nothing is ever as simple as black and white, is it? When an artist paints a portrait of a black chair, does he use only black paint? Everyone has a unique perspective of the world. We receive all information through our five senses: sight, sound, taste, touch, and smell. We use our senses as filters to create and interpret our reality. Your perspectives are based on all the information you have collected your entire life regarding time, space, language, memories, decisions, values and beliefs, and attitudes.

Listen to learn about him. Listen to understand him. Listen to be a great communicator. We think people are good conversationalists because they are genuinely good listeners. Get a clear sense of his values. What is important to him? What does he want? What does he not want? What does he desire? What does he need? What does he love? What does he hate? What must he have? What must he never have? Be authentically interested in what he has to say—listen, listen, listen. They say that's why God gave you two ears and one mouth—we should be listening twice as much as we're speaking. Men trust facts, not feelings. His answers are going to tell you his values and beliefs, which will show how he feels. If you listen closely to his opinions, he is constantly unveiling himself and his feelings. Listen not to agree or disagree with him, but merely to learn more about him. Acknowledge his opinions, showing him you respect him. Learning what is important to him is important to you in recognizing your exceptional man.

As women, we feel more connected by disclosing things about ourselves and about those close to us. This is not the case with men. Men don't divulge information. It's an inherent survival mechanism. At times, you may feel he is shutting you out and not communicating his emotion, but this is a man's way of protecting himself and those he loves. If you want him to express himself to you, you must make it safe for him. He should not feel you are threatening or challenging him, but that you are welcoming him to share his beliefs. A man will not fight for the opportunity to express himself. Don't judge the information coming from him, but simply receive it. Men believe if you disrespect their opinion, you disrespect them. That being said, a man doesn't care if you agree with his opinion as long as you respect it. However, women will feel a disconnect if opinions are not in accord. Women connect by divulging personal information and having our feelings supported by one another. We feel loved when others reinforce our beliefs.

Crown Jewel: Women feel more connected when others agree with their opinions. Not so with men—you needn't agree; merely respecting his opinion is enough.

There are inherent differences in the brains of men versus women, which could explain why women seem naturally more talkative than men—or possibly it could be conditioning after birth. Whether innate or learned, it does seem that girls talk more about their feelings and share their life experiences more than men. Whatever the reason, it seems that very feminine women are habitually more expressive vocally, as well as physically, than men. People fear rejection in expressing their true emotions. I encourage women to fully emote rather than repress unpopular feelings. I continually witness men being extraordinary men when they are in the presence of a feminine emotional woman. This doesn't mean to act inappropriately in any given circumstance, but we have become such a controlled society, core emotions are often suppressed. We have become so regimented at repressing our true feelings that we aren't even aware what they are. Get to know yourself so others can get to know the real you.

Crown Jewel: If a man offers to do something, it means he wants to. He's not like a woman, who will offer just to please others.

A widely known concept is that whenever someone says "I am," it is his or her identity. The person fully associates to whatever comes after "I am." As human beings we must remain consistent with our identity; otherwise, we feel great discomfort. This means we must either be internally congruent with our identity or change our identity. Here is my identity: I am a loving daughter. I am a fantastic sister. I am an amazing friend. I am a successful attorney. I am an intelligent student. I am a well-rounded woman. I am a financially stable member of society. I am a world traveler. I am a terrific dancer. I am a child of God. I am a spiritual being, full of love. These are all things I definitely believe to be true; therefore, my unconscious is constantly making certain I stay congruent with this identity. When I want to change a pattern, I can change my identity to coincide with that new pattern. For instance, in working on my eating habits, I adopted the identity that I am super healthy and love greens.

Try it on yourself and with your friends. Who are you? Who are you at home? Who are you at work? Who are you with your friends? Who are you with your family? Keep answering the questions over and over and uncovering your true identity. This is not about how others perceive you; this is about who you believe yourself to be. We will do whatever it takes in order to remain consistent with our identity. Use the knowledge that you must remain consistent with your own identity to change your habits. For example, if you are "trying" not to be depressed, label yourself as a positive person. If you are "trying" to exercise, become athletic. Literally use the words to define who you are. "I am a positive person." "I am athletic." A man's identity will show you if he is ready for a partner and what he is looking for in his significant other.

Men are mission driven and aren't really looking for a partner until they are well established on their career path. Men are single focused, working on one goal without distraction and then moving on to the next. Women, on the other hand, have diffused awareness and can multitask very well. You may notice a man taking care of his own needs, seemingly unconcerned with your needs, but a man is not taking care of his needs instead of yours; he's taking care of his needs in preparation for taking care of you. That being said, if a man doesn't think he can make you happy no matter what he does, he won't even try. This confused me for years. I would go out with a guy and couldn't understand why, after having a fabulous date, he wouldn't attempt a second. A man typically isn't going to try winning you over if he doesn't wholeheartedly think he can please you in the end. He will conserve his energy for that prize he can win, the woman he truly can make happy. Men are designed to want to please and protect women. Watch their actions and you'll see—even with men who aren't your man. Have you ever had a man help you jump-start your car or fix a flat tire, hold your door or help you lift something heavy? They want to provide for women. It's their true nature.

Crown Jewel: If a man doesn't think he can make you happy in the long run, he won't even try.

You now know how differently men process information. You are aware that men are your reciprocal energy, not your identical self. His energy will complement yours, not mirror it. You have recognized your own identity and know how to determine the identity of others. You know how to engage a man in conversation to bring out his core values and beliefs. When you meet your date in person, you will now be able to determine the chemistry, then move on to assess the fundamental components of a relationship. The exciting part of the date is determining that chemistry, and you already know how to do that. We do it every day, in every interaction. How do we know if we trust another person? How do we know if we want to spend more time with another person? How do we know if we like another person? You listen to your intuition. Trust your gut. When there is chemistry, you know it. It's magical.

Chapter Eleven:

There Are No Rules— Trust Your Intuition

The first rule is: there are no rules. Most importantly, when it comes to making decisions and deciding your course of action, we know to trust your gut. Your entire digestive system is strongly connected to your emotions and state of mind. Have you ever gotten knots before you performed a speech or butterflies when you were around a new love interest? Recently, the connection between the nervous system and the digestive system has become more widely understood. The gut and the brain constantly exchange chemicals and electrical messages. What affects one is directly linked to what affects the other. The gut contains over one hundred million neurons. Neurons are nerve endings that communicate and translate information by chemical and electrical impulses throughout the body. The gut is actually located throughout the tissue lining the esophagus, intestines, colon, and stomach. We constantly confuse the signals from the two brains.

When we experience major tension, we release stress hormones to prepare us for fight or flight. Stress causes the adrenalin production in the gut to increase. Emotional turmoil can cause an overload of this adrenalin, which can induce nausea or ulcers as well as many other ailments in the stomach and throughout the body. Have you ever been in a fight with your boyfriend and gotten physically ill? Adrenaline can accelerate your heartbeat. It also redirects the blood flow away from other vital areas in order to dedicate that blood to the muscles for any necessary protective response. Thus, adrenaline is very beneficial when you need a quick burst of energy for survival. Not only does this additional adrenaline give you a burst of heightened memory and immunity, but it also lowers your sensitivity to pain. Your unconscious controls the adrenaline pumped into your bloodstream. This is why people can triumph beyond human capabilities when threatened. Have you heard the story of a mother lifting a car to save her child? A burst of adrenaline can save your life. On the downside, a perpetual overload of adrenaline creates a burden and can deteriorate your body quicker than anything you consume. Continued adrenal stress on the body causes numerous health issues, including lower immunity, increased blood pressure, impaired cognitive abilities, thyroid malfunctioning, insulin resistance, fat storage, and bone and muscle atrophy. Your gut attempts to keep you even keeled by producing serotonin and dopamine. These neurotransmitters work to keep you calm and stable in the face of difficulties. Almost all chemicals regulating your brain are also present in your gut, including hormones and neurotransmitters.

Crown Jewel: Your gut is your unconscious mind; it's your intuition. The clearer you get, the more you will recognize what your gut's telling you. This is why meditation enhances your intuition.

Your gut is tied to your unconscious mind. Your unconscious mind accumulates and stores all the information you've ever collected. Even if you are unaware of it consciously, everything you have ever been exposed to is recorded in the unconscious mind, also referred to as the subconscious. Your unconscious mind is at work every moment of the day of your entire life, whether you consciously recall something or not. Every piece of knowledge you have learned, everything you have ever read, everything you have ever seen, anything your body has been exposed to is all permanently ingrained in your unconscious mind. Every man who has ever hurt you, every man who has ever loved you, all your feelings associated with men are permanently stored in your unconscious mind even if you do not consciously recall those experiences or emotions.

Your subconscious powers are much quicker and stronger than your conscious mind. When you meet a man in person, your unconscious can determine the chemistry much quicker than your brain. This is why sometimes a man looks great "on paper," attractive and successful, but the minute you meet him, you know he's not "the one." Your unconscious, your gut, your intuition, knows when something is going to happen half a second before your conscious mind becomes aware of it. Your unconscious is not under the direct control of the conscious mind; it operates below your conscious awareness. What this means is that you don't know how much you actually know. If you know how to interpret your gut response, it will tell you what you need to know about a date quicker than your mind can analyze him.

Crown Jewel: Your subconscious mind is all-knowing and much quicker than your conscious mind, so it can give you feedback much faster than your brain can analyze information.

There are four stages of consciousness: unconscious incompetence, conscious incompetence, conscious competence, and finally, unconscious competence. When you are unconsciously incompetent, you are not aware of what you do not know; you don't know what you don't know. When you progress to conscious incompetence, you have now discovered the things you didn't know, but you still don't know how to handle them; you are still incompetent at dealing with them. When you perfect your skills, you become consciously competent—not only do you now know the things you didn't before, but you also know how to handle it, you just have to think about it consciously to make it happen. Once you have consciously mastered how to make it happen and repeat the process over and over, it will become habit, thus you have become unconsciously competent—it's now automatic. Repetition is the mother of skill.

An example of the four stages of consciousness I've recently experienced is that I have been working for some time to change my habit of looking at people's lips when they speak to focus instead on their left eye for a deeper connection. At first, I wasn't aware that I was less connected or even that I was focusing on their mouth at all—I was unconsciously incompetent. Then, after studying body language and rapport-building techniques, I learned the skill of direct eye contact but continued to focus on people's mouths when in conversation—I became consciously incompetent. Next, I started making an effort every time I would become aware that I was focusing on someone's mouth to redirect my attention to that person's eyes—I became consciously competent since I still had to remind myself to break my old habit of looking at their mouth. Finally, I have ingrained the pattern of looking straight into a person's eyes so that it is my natural, automatic response—I am unconsciously competent. The response is now part of my unconscious patterns.

Crown Jewel: You can use the four stages of consciousness discussed above to change any habit you want to. You can "program" your unconscious through excessive repetition to habitually respond in any manner you choose.

At first in learning to focus on a person's left eye, I had to practice, consciously reminding myself over and over again to take my focus off a person's mouth and redirect it to his or her left eye. It took me quite a while to form the habit, thus programming it into my unconscious. It is said a habit is formed in twenty-one days because it takes the unconscious ten thousand repetitions to master a new condition. Your unconscious learns by repetition, not logic. Your unconscious does NOT think or reason; it takes the information you give it and accepts it as true. This means your unconscious is more convinced by hearing or doing something over and over and over than by logical arguments. Use that power of your unconscious mind to make you irresistible to men. Become that positive, happy, feminine woman you were born to be so that when your exceptional man shows up, he will recognize the exceptional woman before him.

This was another tool I used without ever knowing it existed: when I started my self-development spiral upward, I would listen to positive greats like Tony Robbins, Napoleon Hill, Zig Ziglar, Wayne Dyer, Deepak Chopra, and anything else positive I could get my hands on. There is a wealth of useful positive information out there today. Find which one feels right to you and then listen, listen, listen. I would put them on my headset and literally do everything all day listening to this positive reinforcement. I would shop with it on, work in the yard with it on, clean the house with it on—sometimes I would even sleep with it on. For me, the result of this immersion was that it worked my positive muscle so well that it's now my automatic response.

The greater number of times the unconscious is exposed to information, the stronger the pattern becomes. This repetition builds the neuropathways, making the connection between ideas stronger. Neuropathways are created in the brain when nerve endings release chemical and electrical impulses to communicate with one another. I used positive learnings through these master teachers to increase my positive response. The more repetition, the stronger the connection, thus the more embedded the pattern. It's just like working any other muscle in the body; with more repetition, the muscle is stretched and eventually retains its new shape. Be careful; you can also strengthen any negative neuropathways with this same process. This is why it is so important who and what information you expose yourself to. There's a reason people say "who you surround yourself with is who you become" or "be careful what you feed your brain." The more frequently your unconscious is exposed to something, the more ingrained that thing becomes until it inevitably creates a pattern.

This is also why full immersion in any given subject will get you the quickest return at becoming proficient in any area. If you take dance lessons once a week for five years, it's the same amount of time as taking dance lessons full-time for a month. Literally you would spend the same time taking a dance lesson once a week for five years (52 x 5 = 260 hours) as you would taking a dance class 8 1/2 hours a day for a month (8 1/2 x 30 = 255). So technically speaking, you can learn exactly the same amount of information spread out over five years or in one month full-time. You likely learn much more in the month intensive since each time you don't have to relearn forgotten elements from the prior week. This is why actors are able to become experts for a movie in skills they had never before attempted or how, on competitive television shows, people can become experts in a matter of weeks. It's their job. They take it on full-time and study with a teacher who's the best in the field.

Crown Jewel: You can study any subject once a week for an hour for five years, or you can study exactly the same number of hours by dedicating yourself full-time for one month.

Always learn from the best in training to be the best at any given task because those small differences separate the good from the best, second place from first. As Tony Robbins would say, it's the millimeter rule. For example, if you were to charter a boat and started off course by as little as one millimeter, you will end up miles away from your intended destination. Even one millimeter could make the difference between life and death. It's like target practice—if your aim is off even a millimeter, the bullet can hit well outside the bull's-eye. Similarly, the highest-performing athletes beat their opponents by as little as a millimeter. That millimeter gets you the gold. You must learn from the best teacher to reach your full potential. You want to stretch that muscle the farthest it can go for the greatest opportunity for growth. When you fully immerse, the unconscious mind is trained much more quickly. It always does exactly what it's supposed to do; it always takes as true the information you give it. What areas are you good at but want to become the BEST? Fully immerse in those areas and study under the best teachers. In reading this book, you are well on your way—now you must integrate the learnings on a daily basis to ingrain the new patterns.

Crown Jewel: When people say you think in pictures, they are referring to the unconscious mind. It is highly symbolic and takes everything personally.

The purpose of your unconscious mind is to serve and protect. When your gut feels that something is off with a man, it's your body's way of setting off an alarm to warn you of impending danger. The unconscious runs and preserves the body and all of its intricate systems like your heartbeat and breathing, even during sleep. All the mechanics of your body are regulated in perfect order by your unconscious mind. The unconscious at work is exemplified through muscle memory. When you learned to walk, at first it took your conscious attention. Now it is beyond second nature. It has now become your automatic behavior. Think of when you trained to drive a stick shift. At first you had to remember the gas, the clutch, the gears, but now you can perform all these automatically. Driving has now become the habit of the unconscious mind, freeing your conscious mind to perform other tasks. You can talk on the phone, listen to music, even put on your lipstick— all while driving. Your unconscious takes care of the driving while your conscious takes care of the rest. Always remember: safety first.

The unconscious filters all the information coming in through the outside world. Our unconscious mind allows our brain receptors to recognize patterns, which accelerates our understanding, giving us the ability to make conscious decisions. Just as your body has scars from physical injuries, your unconscious has injuries from emotional wounds. This is the "baggage" people carry from past relationships, and sometimes they are even unaware of it. If you are lugging anything unwanted from your old relationships, you now have the tools to change those patterns of thoughts and behaviors. These patterns, or neural pathways, are established from past experiences, which become programmed belief systems. It's how you learned to make external judgments for your survival, but just as you learned them and ingrained them into your unconscious, you can learn new patterns. You can reprogram your unconscious.

Your unconscious mind is the domain of emotions. Your unconscious may even illogically link information. Perhaps as a child you caught tonsillitis right about the time you ate a great big piece of pumpkin pie, and now you hate pumpkin pie. The neural pathways fire and link the information even though there is no real cause and effect connection.

The lag time of cause and effect can also confuse your unconscious, so you do not see the direct connection between events. For example, if you eat a whole chocolate cake, it takes a few days for the extra weight to show up in the form of fat. If we were to see the cause and effect instantaneously, our unconscious would realize the true connection by virtue of the immediate response.

Crown Jewel: Your unconscious is an obedient servant that controls your emotions by virtue of all the information you have ever given it. This information creates internal programming, or habits, which can be changed by reprogramming the unconscious by forming new habits through repetition.

Just as physical repetitions of the body build up muscle memory, the neural pathways build connections by repeated exercise. These reps are not only performed in the gym, they are every little physical movement you make every day in every little muscle in your body. As humans, we repeat patterns—the way we express ourselves in our bodies, our facial expressions, and our hand gestures. We can witness in people emotions expressed through the nuances of their bodies. Most communication is nonverbal rather than through actual words. You can watch a man, without even hearing him speak, and get a "feel" for him. Many movements are generic expressions of emotion, meaning all people display them similarly. Our unconscious already knows how to interpret all these impulsive moves we see in others. When we become clear and tap into our innate unconscious abilities, we will better intuit our own feelings and our response to others.

Strike a Pose—Body Language Says It All

It is widely accepted that 7 percent of communication is words, 38 percent is verbal (tone or pitch, speed, and volume), and a remarkable 55 percent is nonverbal. Nonverbal communication includes your physiology, your posture, breathing pace and depth, skin color (flushing, loss of color, glow, etc.), eye focus, and any minute movements throughout the body. All these nonverbal cues are processed not only by our conscious mind, but by our unconscious as well—here we go back to the gut response.

Throughout your entire life, you've heard the saying

trust your gut. All these sayings are based on the wisdom of the ages. When we finally meet a man in person, we are able to determine the real chemistry because we are now exposed to the nonverbal exchange of information we couldn't witness through other forms of communication. Chemistry isn't just about physical attraction; it's a shared connection that's inexplicable. So, we may not even consciously get why we are attracted to someone, we just know we feel "it."

Crown Jewel: It is widely accepted that 7 percent of communication is words, 38 percent is verbal (tone or pitch, speed, and volume), and a remarkable 55 percent is nonverbal.

A gentleman may make overt mannerisms that your gut will recognize as sincere. For example, we can all tell when a smile is real or fake. That's why the best actors make the most money. The actor can authentically access the emotion and feelings of happiness to create the smile from the inside out. You may not even consciously be aware of it, but a true smile is exhibited not only in the mouth, but in the eyes and throughout the sides of the face, in the cheek and jaw area. In a fake smile, the corners of the mouth are turned upward, and it is typically more asymmetrical than a real smile. Body language is the external, physical actions expressing internal thoughts. As within, so without. The subtlest movements can speak volumes. Watch his face for every micro-movement, any quick, impulsive facial expressions. These unconscious movements reveal his true emotions.

We all know the classic body language clue that folded arms mean the person is not open while upward palms mean the person is. Here are a few more jewels on nonverbal communication: Closed or crossed body parts, including legs or fists, signal defensiveness. His right arm is controlled by his left hemisphere, which is the analytical side of the brain. Opposite is his left arm, which is controlled by his right hemisphere, the creative side of the brain. If he places his left hand on his heart, the move is guided by his creative brain, so it may not be genuine, while the right hand over the heart likely is. If his feet are pointed toward you, he is interested. His hands near his genitals also indicate he is interested. Strong emotions go out the hands. When a man is angry, he may hit something or flail his arms about. If he is tapping or rolling his fingers, he is bored.

Rubbing the nose or covering the mouth is to hide what is coming out of the mouth; he may not be telling the truth. Liars may unconsciously place objects between themselves and their accuser, such as walking to the opposite side of a table or holding something in front of their body. Guilty parties may be uncomfortable facing you and turn their heads or bodies in another direction, again avoiding eye contact. Excessive blinking may also indicate lying. The normal blink rate is twenty per minute. Actors blink about twice as fast. It could be a myth women blink twice as much as men; however, it is certain that women have been known to bat their eyes when in the presence of a potential suitor. A person's blink rate is correlated to his or her psychological arousal. Psychological arousal or autonomic arousal, heart rate/blood pressure, respiration, and skin conductivity, are what the polygraph tests. The eyes may get wider to see more clearly, or lowering the eyebrows and closing the eyes slightly may be an attempt to conceal something. Particularly when the head is lowered, along with other eye postures, it may be to avoid the eye-to-eye contact, which may indicate lying. A guilty person often gets defensive, while an innocent person often gets offensive.

If he is interested in what you're saying, you may see one or several of the following: his hand to his cheek with his index finger extended; direct eye contact; his head tilted; or stroking his chin. If he is nervous in your presence, he may make strange noises like whistling or clearing his throat. Clearing the throat can also be associated with lying. He may also avoid eye contact and expose nervous ticks or fidgeting if he is uncomfortable. People may not be expressing their true emotions if their gestures or facial expressions don't match their verbal statements, like saying, "I'm happy" while frowning. As I explained, fake smiles are limited to mouth movements rather than the entire face. True emotions are not simply expressed in one tiny area of the body; they will be congruent throughout one's entire being. Look to see if his actions match what he's telling you, such as telling you he is committed but leaving his profile active.

Crown Jewel: If he's interested in you, he may point part of his body toward you, raise his eyebrows, hold eye contact, or even touch you.

We know how important conveying confidence out into the world is; making direct eye contact is key. A sense of security and strength is conveyed through the eyes of a confident man. A confident man will typically demonstrate an erect physique along with symmetrical face positioning and body posture. Confident posture will be such that his body is balanced and grounded, with both feet flat on the floor. Slouching, drooping the shoulders and head, wavering, and moving from side to side are indicative of feelings of inferiority or insecurity. Men and women differ in their stance and movement. Feminine women are soft, tending to sway their hips and shoulders. They have much more movement throughout their bodies than men. Masculine men tend to have an erect spine, are very still, and are present with strong eye contact. You can feel the depth and presence of a man when he makes and maintains direct eye contact with you.

The eyes are the windows to the soul. Eyes are significant in determining the meaning of nonverbal communication. They can express your internal feelings and accentuate other facial clues. You can see a man's heart through his eyes. Extended eye contact can make people feel very uncomfortable, or it can make them feel very connected, depending on the context of the relationship. Typically anything over five seconds is an extended gaze. When you are in normal conversation, people generally make direct eye contact except when anticipating their next words. Often, when making this ordinary eye contact, we are actually not looking into the eyes at all, but rather around their eyes and face, possibly even watching the mouth. As I discussed, I realized I often watched a person's mouth in order to better interpret the words I was hearing for clarity. It is a much more powerful tool of connection to focus both your eyes on a person's left eye when communicating.

Crown Jewel: Dilated pupils indicate attraction. If his pupils grow large when he looks at you, he likes you.

All this body language knowledge will allow you to better understand and decipher what is going on internally with your date. Your gut will be your guide. Your unconscious is always doing the work; now your conscious will be able to better access that infinite wisdom. When you finally get to meet him and get up close and personal, you will immediately assess the chemistry and know how to reflect back to him your level of interest. You now know all the subtle ways to flirt with him and how to interpret his response to your flirtation. Remember, it's Groundhog Day every day, so hone your dating aptitude and perfect those skills. On a date, you get to practice your newfound expertise, and you both have a fabulous time—it's a win-win. Not only do you finesse him with your dating abilities, but you may find the opportunity to refine your Ideal Mate List as well. He gets your undivided attention and experiences firsthand all your efforts in becoming your most exceptional you.

Now that you have all the nonverbal moves down, it's on to the exchange of words. You will shortly become the consummate conversationalist, engaging him with your impeccable skills of communication. You now know how easy it is to be a great conversationalist because most of the time you simply spend listening. When you have a genuine interest in what someone is telling you about it will show in your micro-movements. It's as easy to be interested when you find that common ground. Everyone—yes, everyone—has life experiences that are unique and can be of interest, sometimes you just have to dig a little deeper. You have all the rapport skills to engage your date and pull out the most fascinating details of his life. The depth of your conversation and connection is limitless. You have a large pool of men to choose from, don't play in the shallow end, dive in the deep end, because your exceptional man will too.

Chapter Twelve:

What to Talk about on Your Date

So now you're on your date—how exciting. There's no reason to have those pre-stage jitters; you've prescreened, so you know you're going to have a fantastic time. You've fully prepared, so you look and feel absolutely fabulous. You are enchanting and vivacious because you have saved all that energy for your exceptional man. It's time to have some fun and learn about your date. You have been in communication with him, so it's not a totally blind date. You can use all that information you acquired from his profile to engage him in stimulating conversation. Trust your gut to lead you in the right direction in topics of discussion. You will irresistibly charm him with your feminine wiles.

Crown Jewel: Copy and paste (instructions on this in Chapter 8) his profile into an email to yourself. Study the information right before your date so you have perfect conversation starters.

Conversation starters:

Where are you from originally?

Where's your favorite place in the world to travel?

Where's the best place you have ever lived?

What do you like to do in your free time?

What's the most outrageous experience you've ever had?

If you were ten again for a day, what would you do?

What's on your bucket list?

What was the first job you ever had?

What was the craziest place you've ever worked?

What's your definition of successful?

Which qualities do you admire in others?

When do you feel most free?

What characteristics do you think are masculine/feminine?

When do you feel most peaceful?

What does your ideal day look like?

What is your mission in life?

What do you think the purpose of life is?

Do you like to play or watch sports? Which ones?

What would you do with a million dollars?

What's your favorite holiday?

Crown Jewel: Picture yourself watching a movie of you and your date. Is it so boring that it would put you to sleep? Let your energy out to play and have fun.

If you want a better answer, ask a better question. Isn't this true: the better the question you ask, the better the response you get. I use this philosophy throughout my life. Internally, we are habitually asking ourselves questions like: Why is this happening to me? Why did he treat me this way? What did I do wrong? Why doesn't he like me? I have learned that the quality of my questions determines the quality of the responses I receive. Now I look for a more empowering meaning in my experiences. My new questions go much differently: What am I supposed to be learning from this experience? How can I change this situation to better serve? How can I be more of what I want to attract? Any time a challenging situation presents itself, I ask: "What's the lesson? What's the lesson? What's the lesson?" Most importantly, I remind myself that it's just life. You can't mess it up. At any given point in time, you are right where you are supposed to be. In every experience, you are learning the exact lesson you are intended to learn. When you find yourself reacting negatively, ask, "How significant is this in the spectrum of life?"

Crown Jewel: Utilize that handy Groundhog Day technique. If you try questions or comments and get a less than favorable reception, on the next guy try a different tactic.

You may have been instructed never to talk about politics, religion, or exes on a first date. First dates are for learning about your potential exceptional partner, so if the conversation leads you to those areas, there are no hard-and-fast rules; however, some people may get uncomfortable if you approach hot topics. Watch his body language cues and listen to your intuition. You don't want to create controversy on a first date. Remember, as long as you respect his opinions, you don't have to agree with them. Be conscious with your use of language. Use phrases like, "I appreciate," "I respect," or "I agree." Do not use "I understand"; it connotes a negative meaning. Don't use "but"; it negates anything preceding it. For example, if you say, "That is true, but," it negates whatever you have defined as true. You might take a less offensive position by using "and." Rather than tell a date, "a lot of what you're saying is true, but I wonder if you've considered..." try saying, "a lot of what you're saying is true, AND I wonder if you've considered..." This relieves the challenge and generates discussion.

Let your sensory acuity be your guide. Sensory acuity means your awareness of all that is going on around you. Sensory acuity is using your five senses (sight, sound, taste, touch, and smell) to determine an appropriate course of action given the entire dynamics of the situation. It's the physical ability of your sensory organs to receive input. Many people don't pay conscious attention to these sensory cues. Most people live their day-to-day lives in a state of trance. We drive in trance, we watch TV in trance, we eat in trance; many of our habitual routines are done in a state of trance. Have you ever parked your car at work and not remembered pulling out of your driveway? Have you ever watched several hours of TV and not remembered the first show you watched? Have you ever eaten a meal and forgotten what you'd eaten? When we live in a state of trance, we are not present in the moment before us; therefore, we are unable to serve our higher purpose. Don't live in a state of trance. Take note of your surroundings, recognize the experience, appreciate what you feel, and enjoy each speck of time for the beauty it holds. Whether the present moment serves you with enjoyment or lessons, it is always a gift. By being present you are able to tap into sensory acuity and recognize what others around you need from you.

Crown Jewel: There are no hard and fast rules about what to speak of or avoid on dates. Let your sensory acuity—your awareness of the sight, sound, taste, touch, and smell—be your guide.

Some men may not have the advanced sensory acuity skills you have developed. Inevitably, they will ask, "Why are you online dating?" It always baffles me since they, too, are online. I used my Groundhog Day tool to come up with an answer I am really comfortable with: "The Internet is a resource like anything else." I continue on to explain, "I meet guys at the grocery store, restaurants, sporting events, conferences, coffee shops, church—really, anywhere I go. I'm open to meeting men everywhere, and I believe that going online and apps offers a limitless resource in this technological age.

Like anything in life, I'm open to use all the tools available to accomplish whatever goal I am working toward. I find, personally, online dating to be a greater resource than the club scene. At least you have some background information so as to know better your compatibility, and the setting isn't skewed because of intoxication—at least not from the alcohol."

Sometimes a date interrogates me as to how long I've been on online dating, how many online dates I've been on, or if I have any horror stories. I steer the conversation in another direction since I do not feel it is pertinent information and don't want the negative overtone. I truly don't have any horror stories because there are no unsuccessful dates for me. I take the time and effort to prescreen, then trust my gut. I gain valuable insight, even if it's only about my own needs and desires. I reply with something like, "I am choosey about the men I date, irrespective of where I meet them." I also let them know, "I'm an excellent judge of character, and all my dates are lovely regardless of whether we have a *love connection*."

I explain that online dating has been a wonderful way to meet men outside my normal routine. Your exceptional man will admire the positive spin you put on the question.

Crown Jewel: Don't get wrapped up in negative conversations discussing online dating horror stories. Steer the conversation in a positive direction.

Your positive energy always translates into making you more desirable. Everyone wants to be around happy, positive people. Your exceptional man will definitely recognize that positive energy flowing through you, and he will most definitely treat you like the exceptional woman you are. You are a princess and should be treated as such. That doesn't mean you are a spoiled brat; it means you respect yourself and surround yourself with others who respect and adore you as well. Who you spend time with is who you become. Your peers are a direct reflection of the standards you accept for yourself. How do your friends look and behave? Do they take care of themselves? Are they striving for your standard of excellence? You teach others how to treat you, and I am certain you command the utmost respect. I respect myself, and I respect the gentlemen I date. I value his time and money just as I value my own.

I'm a traditional girl, I allow my date to pay, and I express sincere gratitude for whatever he has provided. Just as I always allow men to get my door. Some men may feel emasculated if a woman attempts to pay, while others may appreciate it. I think different generations and cultures have varying views on what is appropriate. I enjoy a man planning a date and his attentiveness to the details during our time together.

I have found you can be too "thankful" with dates. Don't send a follow-up thank you text or call him. Men enjoy making women happy. If you give them too much praise, it doesn't work. I learned this one the hard way with my Groundhog Day approach. I would express so much appreciation for any little thing a man did that it turned him off. I still don't exactly get it, but I know it to be true. Men and women are different; this I also know to be true. Women love appreciation, but for men it can be a turnoff and seem needy if it's overdone. Men love to take care of and protect women. Let him court you. You are an exceptional woman and should be spoiled. I used to have a problem accepting compliments and gifts, not only from men, but from everyone. Now I simply say, "Thank you" and mean it.

Crown Jewel: Don't over "thank" a man; it turns him off. But do flirt; it turns him on.

It's great to be on a real live date. I believe you don't unequivocally know your compatibility till you get in front of your date in person. That's why I don't spend a great deal of time and energy with the messages and phone conversations. They are great screening tools, but to really test the chemistry, you have to get face-to-face. As I explained earlier, consciously he may seem like a good fit. "On paper" he's perfect, but when you meet him, your body may tell you something is off. We often don't know exactly why we are attracted to someone; our bodies experience physical reactions with pheromones and other unconscious responses out of our direct control. There's your unconscious again saving the day. Sometimes, the universe and even our friends are aware he's not our perfect match well before we are conscious of that fact

Chapter Thirteen:

Interactions with Less-Than-Optimal Results

We've all had times when we've built up this fantasy about a guy in our head, only to be disillusioned by the reality of the situation. Sometimes you find that perfect guy, and you just know he is the only man for you. He is so warm and caring, he makes great money, he's handsome—he's perfect. That is "on paper." In reality, he turns out to have some completely incompatible traits, like the guy I dated who hated to fly. Well, I just love to travel. You can see why that one was a problem. It's not rejection; it is the universe protecting you and preparing you for your exceptional man. You never really know what's going on in his life or in his head. Take, for example, the lovely gentleman I met at church. He had the same birthday I did. We all know there are no coincidences; it had to be fate. When I finally got him to open up, I found he was recently divorced and still not over the breakup. It had nothing to do with me; he just wasn't ready.

Don't be hurt when a guy doesn't show you any interest or call you back. It's no reflection on the exceptional woman you are. Frequently in online dating, men disappear after an *indication of interest*, a message, or sometimes even after a great date; this is commonly referred to as *ghosting*. You never know his backstory and how he perceives the world. You have no idea what is really going on in his life or what he is thinking. Don't replay every word pondering whether you could have done or said something differently and ended up with him. Think of this as the universe saving you from an incompatible mate. Since the men online don't have another venue where they will regularly come into contact with you like school or work, there are no ties to break. Don't overthink it; simply enjoy the process of learning about yourself and becoming your most exceptional you.

Crown Jewel: Frequently in online dating, men disappear after an indication of interest, a message, or sometimes even after a great date. Commonly referred to as ghosting. It is no reflection on you. You have no idea of the current circumstances in his life.

Here's some insider information: If a guy feels you are out of his league, he's not going to waste his time on you. As I discussed, a man isn't going to ask you out again if he thinks he can't make you happy in the long run. He is going to save those resources for the woman he can genuinely please. Even if you have a great time on a date, if he doesn't think he can win it in the end, he won't bother trying. Look at it as a lovely compliment. There is a great plan for your life; you are an exceptional woman. You are preparing so your exceptional man will recognize you. These dating exercises are invaluable to your inner development. Water seeks its own level. Like attracts like. When you radiate that exceptional energy you conjure up from within, your exceptional man will be inexplicably drawn to you.

If a guy gets mad at you or sends a nasty message, do not respond. Any time you respond, even if you are attempting to soften the blow, it will stir things up. You may be so incited by his comments that you are dying to express obvious reasons why you would never date him again. Don't do it. Think of what your outcome is. Even if letting him know would help him, would he receive the information from you? Any further contact from you will add fuel to the fire. Most dating sites provide a block feature that prohibits further online communication, though the site may still permit the blocked user to view your profile. If you have a real issue with the user, report your concern to the dating site directly. If you feel threatened, seek outside police intervention.

Crown Jewel: If a guy gets mad at you or sends you nasty messages, do not respond. If you respond, even in a polite way, this will keep the energy building, adding fuel to the fire.

Occasionally, a guy will get aggravated and send derogatory messages due to lack of any reciprocated interest.

Literally, you can make no contact with a member, and he could get angry with you. Some men may have this response after a message, even when you have put nothing objectionable in your note. Remember, everyone sees the world through his or her own perspective, and his glasses may not be rose colored like ours. I have had men say mean remarks, then a month or two later, they are again pursuing me. You never know what is going on in their lives. Maybe his last girlfriend once said something similar; even if it's a positive statement, it may unconsciously bring up negative emotions in him. It's difficult not to let his negative energy affect you, but what other people think of you is none of your business. Don't be at the mercy of another's judgments of you, whether they are good or bad. Don't allow someone else's opinions of you to become your own. You know yourself more intimately than anyone else in the world. You know your true heart.

Most men will know whether there was enough chemistry to feel appropriate asking for a second date; however, if he has poor sensory acuity and asks you on another date, and you do not wish to pursue the relationship further, respectfully decline. You needn't tell him you will go out with him if you have no intention of doing so. Men prefer the truth, even if it stings a bit. They quickly move on. Even though you do not owe him a reason, I commonly feel and use, "I believe we are looking for different things" or "I believe we are at different places in our lives." Ultimately, he should respect your honesty, and it will strengthen his appreciation for the integrity of all women. I know it seems difficult, and you don't want to hurt any of these men, but it's much more considerate not to spend any further time with them rather than lead them on if you don't feel any interest. Your exceptional man is on his way, and you want to be open and prepared for his arrival, not closed because you've been dating men of no real interest to you.

Crown Jewel: If you are not interested in a guy, you owe him no explanation but may use, "I believe we are looking for different things" or "I believe we are at different places in our lives."

You're so Close, Never Give Up

After a not-so-great date, you may feel like giving up— even going back to your ex-boyfriend. Don't do it. With each experience you are growing more and more into an exceptional woman who will attract your exceptional man. Keep pushing forward; your exceptional man's out there. Have faith. A common theme among those on the self-development path is that there are no failures in life, only feedback. Every experience is a learning experience. Thomas Edison spoke regarding his attempts to create the light bulb, "I have not failed. I've just found ten thousand ways that won't work." You are sharpening your skills in the dating arena, and you're one step closer to your destiny with your exceptional man. Each man is a free trial run to put your learnings into experiential lessons. Sometimes the lessons are fun, sometimes not so much. With real growth we must face our own internal idiosyncrasies. The things you find irritating in another may be the exact qualities you find irritating in yourself. Others will be a mirror to us, revealing facets we don't like in them that also reside in us—a reflection of those parts of ourselves we suppress. Are you projecting qualities you don't like in yourself onto someone else?

When people are troubled, they tend to place blame. They blame others, they blame themselves, even events from their past. He may blame you for his hurt because it is easier in the short run than accepting responsibility. I don't blame anyone anymore, including myself. In every situation you are challenged with, ask, "What's the lesson?" This takes a negative and turns it into a positive learning experience. Very often those experiences we believed to be the most devastating times in our lives have turned out to be our biggest successes because of the lessons we or those around us have learned. Let your mantra be, "I am a powerful manifester. I have created everything that surrounds me. I am a powerful manifester. I can change everything in the flash of an eye." You are always at the "cause" of what "affects" you. This gives you the power to determine your outcome.

Crown Jewel: Very often those experiences we believed to be the most devastating times in our lives have turned out to be our biggest successes because of the lessons we or those around us have learned.

I used to spend my life either looking back feeling guilty about the past or worrying about the future, never embracing the present. The present moment is the only experience that is actually real and tangible. People experience guilt when they believe they have violated a moral standard and feel responsible for that violation. I don't feel guilt anymore; it is of no service to me, and it's of no service to you, either. Every experience has led you to the exceptional woman you are today. At that point in time, you made the best decision you could with the knowledge you had. A widely used presupposition of self-development practitioners is that everyone is doing the best they can with the resources they currently have available. A presupposition is an assumption or belief taken as true beforehand. Be grateful for each of those events that have led you to become the exceptional woman that you are and have no regrets on your path to such astonishing self-growth. Take the lesson and leave the guilt. I don't experience remorse anymore; I accept responsibility. I am responsible for everything and everyone I encounter. This allows me to maintain complete control of my life. As a reminder, people are happy in direct proportion to the control they feel they have over their lives. Now that I know I control everything in my life, I can't help but be ecstatic.

Crown Jewel: Don't live your life looking back in guilt or forward in worry. Live in the reality of the moment, the present.

Worry is fear and always relates to a future event—the anticipation of what is to come. Just as with guilt, it serves no purpose. Do plan and prepare for what your future may bring, but don't worry about events that may never occur. People often spend exorbitant amounts of time and energy worrying about events that never come to fruition. Worry leads to stress, and we have learned the havoc stress can wreak on our bodies. Choose to live in the present. The current opportunity for pleasure, change, and growth are all before you in each moment. Being present will allow you to recognize what your gut, your intuition, is telling you and make better decisions. If your outcome is other than what you believed optimal, reassess the meaning. "What's the lesson, what's the lesson, what's the lesson?" I have conviction that everything happens exactly as it is supposed to. Overprepare yourself, then release and go with the flow. You make the effort, have faith, and then trust fate to deliver. And it always does, even if it's not the way you expected it to. You are always given whatever you need for your own evolution.

If I put myself in a situation that is less than desirable, it's my own responsibility. I chose it. I picked my date, and even if he is not my soul mate, I am thankful to have gained clarity in all that I seek in my partner. My Groundhog Day approach allows you to learn on every date, even if it's learning what you don't enjoy. What a gift to have spent the time again refining your Ideal Mate List. I have put myself in every situation, and I can also change that situation in the flash of an eye. Any decision you have ever made that hasn't gotten you what you wanted was your responsibility. But you know what? Every time that happens, you can always, always change it. You can change your state, change the way you are interpreting the situation, or change what you are giving and therefore getting.

If you aren't getting what you want in any given moment or in life as a whole, practice my Groundhog Day approach. Keep changing your tactics till you find an approach that does work. This is a great tip with your entire profile and dating techniques. If you find you aren't having the kind of men you desire soliciting you online, change your profile, change your user name, change your photos, change your autobiographical section. And if that doesn't work, change it again. So, when you aren't getting what you want, first change your state, then use that new state to change your approach. Again, one of the concepts I have found personally useful is the idea that there are no unresourceful people, only unresourceful states.

Crown Jewel: If you find you aren't having the kind of men you desire approach you online, change your profile. Change your user name, change your photos, change your autobiographical section. And if that doesn't work, change it again. It's Groundhog Day every day online.

So you say, "how do I change my state?" The quickest way to change your state is to change your physiology. You can go drink a glass of water, jump up in the air, dance, hug yourself—whatever you want to do to physically change the position you are in. Changing the position of your body will change your emotional state. Put on that external smile and work it from the outside in. Perform some of those activities I mentioned earlier that elevate your mood. Pull out your Happy Times List—dance, sing, love on your animal— whatever it takes. Keep stacking the happy times to intensify your positive emotions. You are an exceptional woman in every moment no matter what state you are in, but isn't it much more fun to be in a great one.

A common fear is: what if he doesn't look like his photos? What if he lied about his height? When a person puts a fake or deceptive profile, it's referred to as catfishing. Again, in your screening process, pay close attention to ALL his photos. Some men will mix in recent pictures with those taken many years prior. I study profiles, including the photos, and then go with my gut. My dates always look *something* like their pictures and are usually within a few inches of the height listed, although I may still not be physically attracted. You know by now that even if I'm not interested, I still have a lovely time. After I've discovered I'm not with my exceptional man, I feel no pressure, no nervousness. It's so much fun to share the experience when you're fully invested and present even absent a chemical attraction. I value the connection we do share; the universe has brought us together at that point of time. You can learn something valuable from each person who's in front of you, even if it's harder with some than with others. It means you must dig deeper within yourself to access that part of them you can relate to. I am continually learning about myself and about the world.

Crown Jewel: "Only what you are not giving can be lacking in any situation"3 (A Course in Miracles).

Another interesting challenge is running into a former online date when you are out with your friends or a date. It is no different than running into anyone else you have dated. Handle it with the poise and class you always do. I have no issue telling people if I met a gentleman online; however, you needn't explain to whomever you are with how you met the gentleman if you are not comfortable doing so. All my girlfriends know I'm online dating, and I know how exceptional I am, so it doesn't bother me a bit. I've even had those funny times when I met someone at an event and just knew I had met him before, only to discover we had connected online. Everyone is doing it. There's no reason to be embarrassed.

Crown Jewel: If you run into an online guy when you're out, there's nothing embarrassing about the fact that you've dated him or even that you met him online; however, if you feel uncomfortable revealing that, you can always use the line so many do: "We met each other through a mutual friend." You don't have to divulge who that mutual friend is.

My advice is never; never have a first date with an online guy at an event with your friends, or even worse, your family. You haven't met him in person to determine the chemistry and whether he matches up to his profile. I know you have good intuition at this point, but why risk it? You want to be proud of the men you choose to share with your friends and family. A first date is to learn about your prospective love interest. Something intimate where you can engage him in personal conversation is ideal. Social settings with friends and family won't provide the opportunity to get to know him more personally. Save those communal dates for when you know you are interested in pursuing the relationship further and want to see how he responds to interactions with your most prized friends and family. Once you get to know him better, you can determine when the timing is appropriate for those introductions. Watch his interactions with people in passing, the wait staff, busboys, and cashiers. We are all interconnected. How you treat anyone is how you treat everyone.

Chapter Fourteen:

Actual Online Date Reviews

This chapter will generalize several types of men I frequently run into out on the town and online. I decided I wanted to learn more about myself, my dating habits, and men. When I decided to approach dating with this newfound purpose, I was so excited to go on the dates with this mission. Not only was I looking for my exceptional man, I was looking for even more of my exceptional self. What an amazing way to learn about yourself and refine your dating skills. Such amazing lessons. Prior to this experiment, I felt I was a wonderful date. I can always find a topic to generate a conversation around. I'm never argumentative and can always empathize with others. But there is so much more to having that depth of connection a man is compelled to pursue. A deep connection with another soul takes more than finding common ground; it's a heart opening led by an exchange of energies that's nonverbal. This goes back to that fact that most of our communication is nonverbally shown through our physiology as discussed in Chapter 11.

Crown Jewel: A man needs to feel that chemistry, as if there is nobody else on earth who can cause that electricity.

One of the most valuable lessons I learned was that before the experiment, my energy on dates had become a bit flat, meaning my energy level showed less than the vibrant, exceptional woman I am. I think dating had become a little routine for me, losing its luster. This new mission made me sparkle again. When I gave myself this new purpose in dating, to discover about myself and my dates, to grow and learn as much as humanly possible on each encounter, that mission provided a new drive, a new outlook, and a new energy. The most profound exercise was when I went on a date immediately after a facial. I didn't realize that my appearance would be so unimportant to my date. You see, the facial made my skin super sensitive, so for several days I couldn't wear any makeup. I was horrified. I almost canceled the date. I usually don't leave the house without at least a bit of foundation powder, blush, and lipstick—not even to exercise.

Something inside drove me to push forward and go on the date irrespective of my appearance, and you know what? Wow, did he respond. I gave it my all. I used all my maneuvers from my Feminine Times List to really get into my body and prepare my energy. After my facial, I went home and soaked in a bubble bath. I danced and sang around the house as I got ready for the date. I put on my favorite lace pink panties and then a super-sexy-classy outfit with the perfect jewelry. When I looked in the mirror, I focused my attention on everything I loved in that moment about myself: the shine of my hair, the line of my dress, and the sparkle in my eyes. Then the final touch—a dab of perfume here and there to lure him closer. It all worked—beyond even my own expectations. My date was a lovely, prescreened gentleman and totally into me despite my less-than-flawless appearance. What an amazing lesson. At any time, what really matters to men is the energy you put forth—the most important thing you bring to the date is your exceptional energy. So, if you're having a bad hair day, spend that much more time gussying up your energy. Looks are not just skin-deep; your beauty goes much further.

Crown Jewel: What really matters on a date is not how you look; it's the energy you bring. All your external beauty is just icing on the cake, and your sweet self is the cake.

Another extremely important lesson was the opportunity to realize that oftentimes as women, we don't radiate our full energy because we fear the light we offer the world. As women, we are often encouraged to become dim, hiding our glorious feminine energy. We are taught that other women will feel threatened by us and men will only want us for "one reason" if we are totally radiant. I personally found that I had become so fearful of my own radiance that I would rather not have men like me as much so that they wouldn't pursue me. I felt it was much harder to be the one rejecting them. I am such a pleaser, and I love to make people happy. All I want to do is share love. I always, always want everyone in a positive state. I've learned that if I hide my true depth and core being, then when I am in front of my exceptional man, he will not recognize me. He will be looking for the exceptional woman who's showing up, and if I'm not radiating how exceptional I am, how will he know? The purpose of a date is to open up and learn about each other, not to put on an act or to be so appropriate that you don't really learn anything about each other. Shine your full radiance so that your exceptional man will recognize you.

For fun, I have included here a few of the varieties of men I've gone out with. These are just a few of the qualities some men possess: Super Dad, The Traveling Salesman, Muscle Man, To the Depths of the Earth, and The Daily Financial. Some men may have none of these characteristics, and some men have all of them plus more. These categories are just to show how any attribute a man has can be fun for you to experiment with in determining whether he's your exceptional man or a lesson along your path. A date could have each of these qualities. He could be a dedicated dad who practices meditation or yoga, goes to the gym on a regular basis, and invests in the market as a hobby while working his day job as a salesman. Each category is exciting and amazing in its own special way, just as each man in real life is distinctly unique and impressive for the creation that he is. No two men are identical; each is a compilation of his thoughts, his experiences, his loves—a collection of various energies in human form. Every man is a life lesson before you, full of opportunities for growth. Learn from them, about them, and with them. It's the game of life; it's meant to be enjoyed. Have fun with all the contestants. There are no rules. There are no losers, only lessons.

Crown Jewel: The game of life is intended to be fun. There are no losers, only lessons. Enjoy each contestant for the amazing collection of energies he is.

Contestant #1

Super Dad

He is faster than a bolt of lightning; stronger than Hercules, and able to multitask like the consummate woman. This gentleman is first and foremost a dad. He can and will do anything and everything necessary to protect his family. He loves his babies and wants to give them the world. He takes it upon himself to make certain they are well provided for, both physically and emotionally. He will move mountains for them. He goes to every game, every parent-teacher conference, and every birthday party. He's there for whatever they need. These tiny tots are well protected by their Super Dad; he is invincible.

He loves all children, but none more than those of his loins. His children's faces light up when he returns home from work. He tells them bedtime stories when he tucks them in. He is intimately involved with every aspect of their lives. This man enjoys being a husband and has proven his ability to maintain relationships. With the first wife, he was young; he still had not grown into the adult he now is. He's looking for his next bride, the one who will be forever. He is more concerned with what is beyond your superficial looks. He knows what fundamentals are necessary for a lasting relationship. Watch out. You might just be his kryptonite.

Contestant # 2

The Traveling Salesman

This is the gentleman who is well put together in posture and appearance. He knows the importance of a first impression and smiles frequently. He exudes confidence and can talk for hours. He's schooled at making small talk or completely carrying the conversation if need be. He's mastered the gift of gab and doesn't often engage in heavy confrontation. He has a great deal of stamina and vitality that push him forward in the face of disappointment, which is part of the game. He is both shrewd and intelligent. He has mastered time management and productivity. He is organized in business and in life. He's extremely charismatic because that's what he's employed to do. He knows how to size up prospects and keep them engaged.

He's got to make the deal, close the sale. He's looking for prospects; he's looking for an exceptional woman. He's learned to get along with all types of people and talk about all kinds of things. He's business oriented but still has a private life as well. He is super social across the board. Generally, he travels a couple times a month for business, staying in the best hotels and taking his clients to all the finest restaurants in town. He's always wining and dining everyone. He is used to such generosity with clients that it extends into his personal life. His patterns of giving have become deeply ingrained; thus, it is his habit to provide for others. He's looking to make a sale, and he's the merchandise.

Contestant # 3

Muscle Man

I am gonna pump you up. Muscle men are extra energetic. This man takes superb care of his physical being. He is well groomed and well dressed. He is extremely conscientious of everything he does to his body. He is personally motivated and into goal setting. He has strong will power and is very controlled. His dedication to discipline shows up in every aspect of his life. He has a strict daily exercise regimen. He spends a lot of time in the gym and outdoors being active. He has learned all the muscle groups and the specifics of how to train each one to its maximum capabilities. He is always looking to participate in some form of competitive sporting event. This man is looking for a "healthy" relationship.

He is high intensity and high energy which translates to high on life. Since I'm a yogi, I always enjoy teaching them a thing or two about flexibility, mentally and physically. It's a great complement to his regimented lifestyle. He eats a lot to maintain his weight and strength; protein is usually a priority. He loves a partner who lives a healthy lifestyle as well, but don't be fooled—he's not typically looking for a stick-thin girl to date; he loves those curves. Not only could you find your exceptional man, but you could have your own personal trainer.

Contestant # 4

To the Depths of the Earth

This man is the yogi of light and a spiritual guru. He loves all animals and all beings everywhere. He treats Mother Earth as if it were his own bit of paradise designed just for him. He is conscious of everything he puts in and on his body temple. His eating habits are often restricted to vegetarian, vegan, or raw. He flows as if he walks on water, appreciating all the beauty nature has provided. He spends equal amounts of time in solitude and loving others. He is full of wisdom and insight on the purpose of life. If he has a question, you need not answer it; he will go within, practicing meditation to seek the answer from the divine. Any time he notices the mental chatter taking over, he quickly quiets his mind in silence.

He is completely supportive of your evolution and offers guidance to you along your path. He is open to all ways and all walks of life. He neither condemns others nor passes judgment. He connects with eye penetration. His calming energy can soothe you without a word. He has little need for pleasure from tangibles; he is more concerned with the pleasures of the body. He loves to light up your senses with smells of incense and perfumes, sounds of the didgeridoo or rolling waves, and visuals of beautiful art or tapestries. His need for worldly "stuff" is limited; he has no attachment to earthly possessions. He longs for world peace and equality. This yogi of light might just light your world on fire.

Contestant # 5

The Daily Financials

You look like a million dollars, and this guy knows it. This gentleman is an accountant, banker, or stockbroker. He has an all-numbers, no-nonsense drive. He watches Wall Street from dawn till dusk. He has an amazing ability to make money count. He has a secure nest egg and is always planning for what the future may bring. He is very disciplined and spends his time and money wisely. He's prepared for that rainy day, should it ever come. He is as hardworking and honest as the day is long. If he tells you he's going to do something, he gets it done with precision and on time. His appearance is very orderly, and his life is very organized. He is meticulous in his attention to detail. He is proficient at cost-benefit analysis and knows when things are worth investing in. He's always weighing the options to make the best decision. He is super smart and stimulated by other intellects. He loves the opportunity to shut his brain off from time to time as well. During those times you may find him redirected and refocused, possibly on sports, possibly on you. You've got a great portfolio, and he's seen it. He may want to manage your assets.

The Fantastic Five

Again, let these just serve as examples of a few of the wonderful qualities some men possess. There is power in noticing patterns in the men you are dating, and there is power in noticing your own patterns in the types of men you are repeatedly attracting and attracted to. This isn't a good or bad thing; it's not a matter of right or wrong. This is personal preference and opportunities for growth. This is why dating is invaluable to your becoming an even more exceptional woman. Have fun, enjoy all your dates, and let your soul grow. You are a magnificent being with super powers.

Chapter Fifteen:

Finding a Keeper

Once you've started dating a suitor, the two of you may be tempted to continue viewing each other's profiles. You may question your recollection of things you read. Did he want several children? Is he politically active? Did he say he loved animals? As I suggested, when you are preparing for a date, you should copy and paste a date's profile and email it to yourself. If you keep information handy, you will not need to continue to view his profile online. As I mentioned, every time you open his profile, it shows under the feature that allows him to see who has been reviewing his profile, and men check this regularly. You can also see who's been visiting your profile to determine whether he continues to view your profile as well. He may be checking to see if you are still active online. This may signify to him you have not stopped dating other men.

There have been times that I started dating a gentleman, and we discussed taking our profiles down. Is the question whether should I take down my profile? Or is it really whether we are a couple? Have you both determined that you want to see each other exclusively? Are you looking to freely date or to pursue a committed relationship? If it is an exclusive relationship you seek, then you must choose a partner seeking the same. If you get obsessed with one guy who's not interested in a committed relationship, you are in a self-destructive pattern. Putting pressure on a man is never the answer. Indicate what you long for, and if he is your exceptional man, he will step up and meet your needs; otherwise, you must remain open for when your exceptional man appears. If a man states in his profile or in person that he is not looking for a relationship, don't think you are going to be the woman to alter his ways. You should take that man at his word. When he tells you what he wants and what he's looking for in life, believe him. Don't try to change him. While it's true that every man is at his best with an exceptional woman backing him, it's because his woman is supporting his full potential, not changing his core being.

Crown Jewel: If a man states in his profile or in person that he is not looking for a relationship, believe him.

See a man for who he is, not what you want to mold him into. Most women are looking for a man who possesses the traits of the consummate woman. As I mentioned, men and women are very different. Women frequently compare themselves, and their men, to what they believe an ideal woman consists of—the intuitive life force that always remembers, is constantly multitasking, and fills up everything and everyone. This is why they are continuously more concerned with others' needs above their own and expect men to be similarly aligned; but men take care of their immediate needs first, in preparation for taking care of others. Women look for a man who thinks like that ideal woman, but they want those masculine qualities in addition. Feminine and masculine qualities are polar opposites; that's how they complement each other so beautifully. A masculine man isn't going to possess the qualities of the ideal woman. He commonly forgets and craves freedom. He is goal oriented and directional, focusing on one task at a time, and he wants to make things smaller, bringing them to completion.

Everyone wants to be loved for the person inside, not for whom someone else wants him or her to evolve into. Don't you want to be loved for exactly who you are, right this moment? Don't you want someone to appreciate all of you, including your idiosyncrasies? Aren't you yearning for unconditional love? You should assess the character of a man, his moral code, not merely his preferences. Your fundamental values and beliefs are essential and should be in line, but personal tastes are custom to each individual. If he has all the qualities that are "must" to you and none of your "must nots," maybe you have found your exceptional man.

Crown Jewel: In picking your man as well as picking your disagreements, "pick your battles." This reference comes from the military strategy suggesting that when troops are thinly spread, they are often unsuccessful. What issues are of real importance?

Once you start dating a man you meet online, you may want to address the inevitable question that will come up when the two of you are together: "How did you meet?" Some men I have been out with are totally comfortable telling others we met through a dating site, while others are less at ease with admitting it. If they ask my discretion, I accommodate, as it matters not to me. I'm proud of who I am and how I use the resources around me, but I respect the fact that he is not. It is courageous to online date, and you should be proud of yourself as well, but if you are not comfortable releasing that information, again you can always tell people you met "through a mutual friend" or on a "blind date." You needn't reveal the source of the connection. If you've found your connection online, if you've found a keeper, that's fantastic. And if you're ready, you can take the relationship offline. There may be other times when you want to go offline as well.

You Don't Always have to be "On"

You don't want to find you've become a serial cyber dater. Sometimes people get addicted to the variety of constantly engaging new people. They go on endless first dates, but never a second. If you are serious about finding a partner, you must look beyond the excitement of the initial response and further into the potential of that partner. You don't want to be so caught up in the thrill of the idea of a "perfect" match that you lose sight of the reality of the men before you. It's easy to get so wrapped up in the illusion of the "perfect" partner that the minute a date does something unanticipated, we are on to the next. Have there been times in your life when you met a person and were less than thrilled to befriend them—then later you found this person was the best friend ever? Don't miss out on your exceptional man because you are distracted by the sea of potentials. You could keep treading water for the rest of your life—missing the boat. If you find yourself in a dating cycle, a pattern that's not serving you, pull out that Groundhog Day trick and change your approach.

You never want to get to the point at which you become jaded with online dating or men in general. Take a break if you need one; conserve your energy for its best use. You want to have all the gusto you need to bring forth when you meet your exceptional man. Take the time to rejuvenate yourself. If you're not at your peak, he may not recognize you at first. Everyone needs to recharge his or her battery at times. That's what sleep is for, and it's why people meditate or stay home to read a book, or whatever works for you. Even exercise, though it is expending energy, helps rebuild it. Think of when you were a kid in school after recess. Weren't you full of energy after you returned inside? Hang out with friends with high energy or a crowd with high energy. I find attending concerts or church skyrockets my energy. Do whatever it takes to change your state and change your energy to meet your full potential as the exceptional woman you are.

Crown Jewel: You never want to get to the point at which you are jaded with online dating or men in general; conserve your energy for the best use.

If you're in a rut, take a hiatus and regroup. Use the time to cultivate energy inside yourself. I never want to miss a thing, but I find if I do everything, I can't do anything full force. There's just not enough energy to go around. It is a less enjoyable experience for me and those around me if I engage in an activity with less than my full pizzazz. It takes the fun out of an otherwise exciting event if I have no stamina to enjoy it. The thing I've learned is that regrouping my energy is also fun. I totally treasure my own company. I love a day at home entertaining myself with a good book or an old classic movie. Even just puttering around the house is a day well spent. I don't always have to be out engaging in the "experience of a lifetime." The purpose of life is to be happy and to connect. Enjoying your own company and connecting with yourself will enhance the experience when you choose to engage with others. If you fully love yourself, you will be overflowing with love to offer others.

There have been times I decided I needed a break from online dating. It can be exhausting when you feel you are only giving energy and not receiving the positive recharge from your date. Be wary of those vampires looking to suck your energy. I have found that people who are down either come up when they are around you, or they suck life right out of you. If you can't bring someone up, he or she will bring you down. As I mentioned, it's just like those tuning forks. People vibrationally align to those around them. To come up they have to want to do the work themselves. They can't simply steal your energy. I love to help people and share all the resources I have discovered, but they have to do the work. You physically can't do it for them. Listen to your gut and take care of yourself. If it's time for a sabbatical from dating, hide your profile until you have restored your energy. When you are ready, you can simply reactivate your profile. This is not time wasted; it's precious time spent loving yourself so your exceptional self is fully nurtured. As I discussed, most online dating sites will allow you to merely hide your profile until you are prepared to resume online dating. So that means you won't have to re-create your profile—simply reactivate or unhide it when you're ready. You can take a break from cyberspace to venture out into the offline world without having to redo all the work when you're ready to return to inner space.

Crown Jewel: Most dating sites have an option to allow you to temporarily hide your profile without having to close your account. This option is normally the click of one button to take the profile offline or hide it, and then one click to reactivate the profile, assuming any subscription fee is current.

Tips for Finding Your Winning Man Offline

While you are online dating, don't forget about alternate resources for dating. Your exceptional man could come from any direction. Don't close any door. Keep your energy up at work, school, conferences, church, weddings, dinner, clubs, malls, grocery stores, gyms, sporting events, parties, art exhibits, and even at the post office. Here's a favorite of mine: shopping at the hardware store. Ask a cute guy to help you find a nail in a haystack. Just kidding, but really ask him to help you find the superglue. You always need extra superglue, right? Frequent the same places over and over; you become more attractive to people with greater repetition. The more exposure, the better you look. Literally, the greater the number of times they see your face, the more attracted they are to you. Stun them with your beauty over and over. Familiarity makes people comfortable, and it builds rapport; therefore, we become more attractive without changing a thing. Have fun playing with all the techniques you have learned in this book. It's not about being needy; it's about being open.

Crown Jewel: Keep yourself out there. Don't seclude yourself in the cyber world. Keep yourself open to meeting prospects everywhere you go.

Keep putting yourself out there in every arena possible. Let your friends and family know you are open to introductions. The more prospects your reach, the more sales you make. Make certain you are using all your tools. Let all that feminine, positive energy ooze from your body. Talk to men in passing, make eye contact with complete strangers, and smile at everyone. Breathe deeply into every cell of your body. Move your hips and your shoulders, wiggle your fingers and your toes. You are full of life. Let it out. Move the world. Use all of your everyday life opportunities to grow into the exceptional woman who will attract her exceptional man. Practice, practice, practice. Men can't help but respond to the energy of a radiant woman—a stranger may simply bask in her radiance. It's not about being someone other than yourself or behaving inappropriately, it's about letting your true core being out to fully live. Even if you get a little too much attention from a guy who may not be your exceptional man, isn't that more fun than receiving no attention? As Mae West said, "It is better to be looked over than overlooked." Again, safety first. Trust your gut, and don't practice these techniques in areas or on men that don't seem safe. When you do notice these exceptional men who are already all around you, enjoy it and appreciate them.

While you are searching for your exceptional man, start rejoicing in the great men already present in your life. In reality, marvelous men are everywhere in your day-to-day life. Some you may know; others you may come across in passing. Some may be your father, your brother, your friend, your colleague, your doctor, your preacher, or even your mechanic. Take note of every gentleman who opens a door for you, every wonderful man who lifts something for you, every great man who asks, "Can I help?" Admire men all around you just being men. What a remarkable creature he is, that his purpose in life is to help women and make them happy. Men are constantly looking for ways to be of service to women; it's how they are built. Isn't life splendid when you are able to appreciate everyone for all they add to the world? Acknowledging those amazing men already present will bring even more exceptional men into your realm.

Crown Jewel: Sing the praises of exceptional men all around you. This energy will attract more of the same.

It's not about whether their efforts help you or not. The fact that they are designed to want to take care of and protect women is astounding to witness. When I fly now, I never lift my carry-on into the overhead bin. I look to the nearest man, and before I can get the words out of my mouth, he has his hands on my bag, lifting it above my head into the bin. The only words I utter are, "Thank you so very much." Practice acknowledging men for the amazing contribution they are to the world and to you in particular. The more you appreciate others, the more others appreciate you. Isn't it true with your friends? The more you love them to pieces, the more they love you. And the love gets bigger and bigger. The more you appreciate men, the more they appreciate you. It's the law of cause and effect. It's just like my positive spiral upwards.

Positive energy builds even more positive energy. Positive energy can be found all around us, in everybody and everything. Just look at who and what is surrounding you. I have found my friends have amazing energy and support my online dating, which makes me even more proud to be writing this book.

Chapter Sixteen:

What My Friends Say about My Online Dating

You are whom you hang around, just as you, my friends, are a direct reflection of who I am. There's a reason people always say "be careful who you hang out with." Who you surround yourself with is whom you become. You're typically drawn to friends you are like or those you want to be like. WOW, do I hang around with some exceptional women. They set the bar high. They won't let me get away with things; they hold me to the highest standards. My best girlfriends are extremely bright, witty, loving, giving, and successful.

I asked each of these women for their feedback on online dating. I wanted to know what they really felt about online dating, no filters. I was shocked at how many of them had personal experience with online dating and how open they were to the idea. This goes back to the peer pressure I had been imposing on myself, believing others would look down upon the fact that I had chosen to online date. Not only were my best friends not embarrassed for me, they actually encouraged my efforts and were proud of me for going after what I really wanted. I was so excited to learn what they thought of cyber dating that I decided to ask a couple of my guy friends what they thought. What insight to go into the male psyche to learn what they think about online dating.

Here are the questions I asked my closest friends:

What do you think about online dating in general?

What do you think about the fact that Drea has chosen to online date?

What is your personal experience with online dating?

Have you ever online dated?

Would you now consider it for yourself?

Why did you choose to date online?

Do you/would you admit to other people that you were dating online?

How does it compare to offline dating?

Where would you suggest going to meet eligible men?

Where did you meet your man?

Anything else you would like to add?

She said...

Audience Member #1

The Renowned Professional Singer & Sensational Mom

I think online dating is a wonderful way to reach out to

a group of men or women you would never have the opportunity to meet in the traditional way of dating. As Drea's friend, and knowing what her wants and needs are, I think this is the best way for her to sift through the men who do not share her interests, yet allows her to explore a variety of men who do, from any location. I personally don't have any online dating experience; I was also married for a very long time. If I were not in a committed relationship at this time, I definitely would explore the possibility of online dating. I sure would admit to online dating. I think it shows character and that you are willing to explore all possibilities and options to find that perfect match. I know several people who met their partners online.

Who really knows where to meet eligible men, seriously? As a musician, I have performed at probably every place in question—church, country clubs, bars, nightclubs, weddings, corporate functions, and conventions. There have been men at all of these places, and although I may not have met the man of my dreams, who's to say he wasn't there. I met my man in Las Vegas. LOL. I think online dating opens the door for many to possibly meet their soul mate. It gives so many more options and choices you don't have dating offline. Of course with meeting anyone, you have to be cautious and sometimes discrete until you know it's someone you'd like to explore and get to know. Even if you don't find love, you may be lucky enough to find a really good friend out of it, and you know what that leads to—his friends, and his friends, and his friends. You get my point.

Audience Member #2

Master's in Marketing, Real Estate Mogul

Online dating is a great alternative to meet people. So many people are dating online now, and I think it's fine that Drea's one of them. I have dated online for several years, off and on. I have met some great guys who have become good friends, but haven't met the right one yet. I chose to date online because the bar scene gets old, and people are trying to squeeze so many things into their daily lives that being able to relax at home in front of a computer and read profiles and see photos of many potential men is sometimes easier than spending several hours out. On an evening out you may meet several men you would be interested in seeing again, or you may meet none at all. I tell my friends I am dating men I've met online, in fact many of them are dating online as well. I do think there is more of a disconnect with online dating because men are more reluctant to take someone out for a long evening if they have never met them before. Some of my best long-term dates were met through my friends. I'm still single and I would encourage someone to try online dating if they haven't before.

Audience Member #3

The Professional Speech Pathologist & Master Mom

I am OK with online dating. Why not? You meet people at bars or a blind date, so why not over the Internet. I have done it. My mom gave me a three-month subscription for my birthday as a gag gift. Honestly, then I was too scared to meet anybody else but liked being able to see what was out there. I am proud of Drea for doing it. Good for her for knowing what she wants and not wasting time with those people who don't have it. She is happy and secure with her online dating, so why not. I feel those people who say they wouldn't do it are too insecure and scared of the rejection. I met my husband through a mutual friend. My only advice would be to go out with anyone once. Go out not looking for a man, and you will find him. I did. Enjoy yourself, continue to be yourself. I love Drea like a sister. I'm so proud of her.

Audience Member #4

The Mindful MBA Real Estate Specialist

In regard to online dating, I think it's hard to tell whether the person is your type from a picture and a bio. It seems like a lot of work. It's a means to an end. You want to find the right man and so are using all venues. I went on one online date. We met for a drink after chatting online for a few days. He wasn't my type at all. I ended the date early and then got bombarded with crazy text messages for a while. Clearly, not the most stable of individuals. I probably wouldn't consider it for myself again. I did it before because I was uninvolved and bored at the time, and I had a few friends who were doing it ;-) I wouldn't really admit to other people I was online dating—only to very close friends. It's hard to read chemistry online. I would suggest meeting eligible men at parties, networking events, classes, fundraisers, and happy hours. I met my man at a party. I'd love for Drea to share on how to not to become jaded when online dating. I have a few friends who are scarred from the experience.

The Prestigious Private Practice Dentist

I like the idea of online dating; it allows you to be proactive and meet people you would have never met otherwise. I have never done it because I am under the delusion it would be exposing me too much. However, I think I will do it soon. I am proud that Drea has chosen to online date. I have no prior online dating experience. I would consider it for myself for sure. I like to go to places and events that I am interested in; those are the places you can meet guys with the same interests as you (church, yoga, classes, etc.). I have met many men in my Poetry class :)). I believe praying for the right man to show up gives you peace, and I swear it works; it opens you up. Pray and take action to be out there.

Audience Member # 6

The Marketing Entrepreneur & Self-Development Guru

Online dating is the way of the future. Generally, I think it can be tricky, sifting through so many profiles and knowing which choices are best. For most of us, I believe dating time is limited. My thought is basically this: online dating opens up a huge range of dating opportunities. Without some "strategy or game plan" you could spend (WASTE) a whole bunch of time there, either wading through countless profiles OR spinning your wheels on dating that goes nowhere. The upside to online dating? The same answer: it opens up a huge range of dating opportunities. I think there can be an element of safety to address here as well. I'm sure that most "applicants" are coming from the right place, and yet, while I've not personally heard of any stories, I would imagine that danger can be lurking. Choosing wisely, meeting in appropriate places, cautiously sharing personal info early on, should be an important consideration when online dating. I think it's a smart decision for Drea to date online. I think that dynamic women, especially, need to venture "out there" to find an amazing partner. Why just shop the neighborhood when the world is your oyster?

Seriously, I've had a blast with online dating, but I have a very open mind, and I find something of value in each person I meet, even if it's to use each experience to get closer to knowing the kind of man I really want. Sure, I've had some sh*** dates and many dead ends, as I have never pursued for any length of time anyone I have met online. Keep in mind that my online dating experience hasn't been within the last twelve years. I'm sure much has evolved since then, in terms of the kind of people who are now turning to online dating. If I wasn't in this relationship, you bet I'd be online dating. I think it's an exciting time to meet so many people. It used to be that we had to find "that right and perfect person" in our own backyard, basically. Now we can shop around the world, and how cool is that? Before I married, and in the "early days" of online dating, I already had the curiosity about who I might find "beyond my normal reach," but I am intrigued by people, and men, and was seeking ways to know a huge expansion of people. Online dating was the only way to really explore—no Instagram/Facebook back then, no social media, etc.—one online dating site was it. Times have changed.

I would absolutely admit to others I online dated. I wouldn't hide it now, and I didn't hide the fact then. I was very open and proud that I had no fear of meeting people or of putting myself out there. It takes a bit of courage to "offer yourself up" and then wait to see if anyone finds you interesting and attractive. I think way back when I was online dating, it was seen as an act of "desperation," a sort of "what's wrong with you, that you have to put yourself on the Internet to get a date?" I think that view has changed considerably. I think it does remain a place for lonely people trying to find companionship, but I also find that the adventurers-at-heart are finding it a great place to meet people and experience another component to LIFE. I found my man when I reconnected on Facebook and then met at a class reunion. How's that for a typical story from the dating world of today? I wholeheartedly encourage Drea to date online. It's a whole new facet of modern life.

He said...

Audience Member #7

The Daring Dentist & Fiancé

Online dating feels like it's safe, and definitely worth

the time and effort. I like the fact that Drea has chosen to online date. I feel it's one of the best ways to date as a professional. My personal experience with online dating was positive. I used a service that directly matches you based on screening questions. You don't search yourself. I considered online dating because I moved to a new city, and I didn't know anybody. I thought it better than going to bars alone or cold approaching women at, say, the gym or grocery store. I totally admitted to others I was online dating. It's slightly different than offline dating. I'm not sure how women should meet eligible men otherwise. I met my woman at a group dinner. The funny thing is, my now-fiancée was one of the matches sent to me on the online dating service I was using, but we didn't put it together when we met since we actually met through friends. We later figured out that we had been matched by the online service. I guess they got it right after all.

Audience Member #8

The Online Business Developer & Newlywed

I think online dating works because people can match themselves up. You can know a lot about the person before you meet, but then it does not work when people lie on their profiles. I went out on several dates. Several women were as much as fifteen years older and twenty to fifty pounds heavier than their profile. I can only imagine that men do the same.

Women usually expect the man to pay. I would suggest meeting the woman at a coffee shop on the first date to make sure that she is what her profile says. The good thing about online dating is that the woman will talk to you because a lot of times women are closed, and it's hard to approach them. For example, if you see a woman in a coffee shop or supermarket, you don't know if she is available and if you should talk to her and what her situation is, whereas in online dating, they are saying they are available. I think it is great that Drea has chosen online dating if it's working for her and it is making her have joyful experiences. I didn't meet my woman online; I met her through a friend of mine. It was more of a friendship at first and evolved into a romantic relationship. I think the best way to meet people is to involve yourself in your hobbies, passions, and events so that a potential lover would have similar interests. For example, if you are into yoga, it would be a good idea to go to a yoga retreat and/or conference on a topic that you really like.

Audience Member #9

The Stock Broker Officer & a Gentleman

I'm a fan of online dating. It's like shopping at the grocery for what you want. You can actually search out ideal qualities rather than getting the luck of the draw at some place like a bar. Sure, you can meet someone in another place like participating in one of your hobbies, but online dating is more likely. Good for Drea for online dating. I've used online dating and haven't had any success, but I am still trying. I have had hit and miss success but nothing solid just yet. I actually found my last girlfriend on Facebook. She was a friend of my sister in high school and I didn't know her, but she knew me.

When she added me as a friend I asked her out, and we had a great time and dated for two years. I'm currently on two well-known online dating sites, looking to find someone I want to spend my life with. I think I have a better chance of finding the woman I truly connect with here than at a bar. There is also a chance to meet her with my social network, but that hasn't happened yet. I admit to others I date online; I am not worried about it. I think the stigma related to online dating has changed. It's no longer like the old personal ad in the newspaper. Offline dating is nice because you know right away that you have connected, and you set up another date immediately as opposed to the messaging waiting game going back and forth. I believe you can meet women at the bar, or riding a bike at the beach, or some similar hobby that you enjoy.

What Your Audience Means to You

These men and women could be your best friends. Friends are intended for love and support. Your standards are in accord with those you surround yourself with. Jim Rohn, a great self-development thought leader said, you are the average of your five people you spend the most time with. If you're finding that those around you pull your energy down on a continual basis, you may need to consider whose company you are keeping. If you are a loving, supportive friend, you will invite other loving and supportive people into your life. I love, love, love my friends and want to see them succeed at everything—most importantly, being the exceptional person they already are. What do you aspire to? What are your deepest desires? If you want it and are willing to do the internal work, there is nothing that can stop you from achieving. Let there be no limit on your capabilities and no limit on your love—you can do anything.

Chapter Seventeen:

Finding Your Happiness

Can you believe it? After searching all my life, I finally realized it—BOOM. One day while in the process of writing this book and getting everything I've ever learned down on paper, it occurred to me that I was special. I don't mean like normal special, I mean like exceptionally special, as are each of you. It's all about growing into that woman I needed to be to attract in all the people and circumstances in life to make me whole. I was well established on my path to becoming an exceptional woman. I saw tremendous depth in myself, which I greatly admired. I respected myself, and more importantly, I found I trusted myself, as a strong woman, to guide myself. I noticed the work I had actually done on myself. I have blossomed into the exceptional woman I was born to be. I now was expressing love for all the parts of myself and loving all the parts in others, without judgment. My life was a reflection of the self-appreciation I had cultivated over the last decade.

I hadn't noticed the process of evolution from the beginning of my self-development journey. I had just been plowing ahead on my own path. I hadn't noticed all those trials and tribulations, my steps backwards to allow me to leap forward. I had been so focused on doing the work. I have tremendously improved every area of my life and those around me are a direct reflection of that self-growth. I'm not talking about people who are there for you; I'm talking about a community who takes your life to another level. Those people that allow me to be vulnerable and really reveal my core being, that level of trust at which I could bring forth the good, the bad, and the ugly, and they would still be right there. If I were hurt or frustrated, they wouldn't run. Isn't it true that everyone wants to be loved unconditionally? The more you give unconditional love, the more you receive it in turn. It's that rule of cause and effect we will cover in more detail later in this Chapter. Also called karma, or in biblical terms, you reap what you sow. Holding onto your love will never get you more of it. The more you give, the more it grows. The more you put out love to everyone, the more it comes back to you from everyone.

We all want love from our family, from our friends, from our community, from our partner. I created My Ideal Mate List with intention, to locate that partner I believe could reflect that love back to me. When we love, it is just that, a reflection back of the love we harbor within. As within sow without. My Ideal Mate List was an expression from the bottom of my heart. It was all those values that were most important to me, but I realized I had been doing my searching for a mate from my head, not my heart. Well, my head may be driving the car, but if my heart isn't beating, we're not going anywhere. It was why I hadn't married any of my past boyfriends, or even my fiancé. It was why I had remained single. My heart was longing for the real deal, a connection so beyond what I was allowing myself to experience with these men I hadn't totally trusted.

Crown Jewel: Your head may be driving the car, but if your heart's not beating, you're not going ANYWHERE.

I had dated plenty of men who looked great "on paper," but that paper wasn't my Ideal Mate List. It was more like looking at a gentleman's resume, with everything in perfect order. I had all these fantasies about how my life was supposed to look and exactly how things would be. I had created these fantasies from things I had seen in movies or on television, things that weren't even what I wanted, but those patterns were ingrained in my unconscious. I believed my future had to look exactly like those people who turned out happy in the movies. These perfect love stories are wonderful to stimulate your creativity, but don't get trapped in that story and lose sight of what you want. What's your goal? What do you really want in your partner—and in life? Visualize your "happily ever after" and tailor it specifically to your deepest desires. Visualize it over and over again so that not only your conscious mind yearns for it, but more importantly, so that your unconscious, which guides those elements out of your immediate control, commands it.

Crown Jewel: You create your reality; it's your script to write. The only story you have to live by is the one you choose. Don't be at the mercy of mainstream opinions.

In traveling around the world alone, I found it doesn't really matter as much where I am, and not even necessarily what I'm doing, but it's who I'm with that makes all the difference. Isn't it true that anything can be fun with the right person, but nothing can be fun with the wrong one? You can have everything you want—a super yacht, a mansion, and a jet—but if you're doing it alone or with someone you aren't connected with, you'd rather be somewhere else. "Stuff" gives you a burst of feelings for about two seconds; deep connections give you those feelings forever. You share the experience, then you forever share the memory of the experience. That warm feeling lasts a lifetime through your memories. Don't you love to sit around and reminisce about your favorite vacation? Remember, your mind thinks in pictures so when you recall an event, good or bad, your body experiences the feelings as if you were reenacting that reality. Sometimes I even find recalling the event in my mind can excite me more than the original experience. I don't have to worry about the logistics or if it's going to work out. Just the thought of things I've done in the past and might even do again in the future gets me totally excited.

Those people I share my life with are my life. I've discovered that for me personally, an experience has little meaning without someone to share it with. It's like viewing the Mona Lisa alone. It's a beautiful painting; you see it and appreciate it for a moment then move on, but if you view that work of art with your best friend, you share an extraordinary experience. You discuss the artist's creation and the effects of her enigmatic smile. Then you're having cappuccino with that same friend weeks later, still relishing in the shared experience. It's a gift you keep on giving yourself with the enjoyment of the memory. This is why memories are priceless: they keep on giving and giving each time you allow yourself the pleasure of remembering. It's the exact opposite of how you use memories in guilt, and isn't it much more fun.

My work on myself has led me to know the purpose of my life. As I have expressed, I believe the fundamental purpose of life is to connect with ourselves, with others, with animals, with nature, with everyone and everything. Connection begins at home, with ourselves. If you don't love and appreciate yourself, how could you expect another to love and appreciate you?

If you don't know how to be happy with yourself, how can you be happy with others? I believe we are put here to have fun and enjoy life. That doesn't mean we don't have trying times, but these challenges are to make us even better people. The difficulties promote our soul expansion. They stretch us so that we grow beyond our own self-imposed limitations. I am so gratified to learn how unlimited our potential in this realm is; I am excited to see how that potential unfolds. Whatever happens next, I am clear in my awareness that I am right where I'm supposed to be, doing exactly what I'm supposed to be doing, learning the exact lesson I am intended to learn in this very second. Do the work and have faith that your higher power will provide guidance in the next step, wherever that may lead.

Crown Jewel: Do you know the purpose of life? What guides you? Listen to your infinite wisdom.

This guidance will lead you in every area of your life if you allow it—listen attentively to your infinite wisdom, your intuition. In studying all the best philosophies in life and aligning them with my scientific beliefs, I have learned that everything—yes, everything—is energy. People are energy, objects are energy, sound waves are energy, light waves are energy, and most importantly, thoughts are energy. Everything in our environment, whether living or inanimate, is infused with movement. It is scientifically proven that objects and elements are made up of molecules, which are made up of vibrating atoms. These atoms are constantly in motion, unseen by the naked eye but greatly affecting our daily lives— because you are energy, anything you do has a ripple effect out into the universe. Your actions or thoughts cause a change in the energy field around you, and that ripples out and touches everything and everybody in the universe; therefore, nothing is unaffected, including its rippling right back on you while building momentum from others' energy along the way.

So, the energy you put out comes back to you even stronger. It's the law of cause and effect. It's karma. What comes around goes around.

Every spiritual practice has principles teaching the universal law of cause and effect. Even science teaches that for every action there is an equal and opposite reaction. Karma beliefs are practiced by Buddhist and Hindu. Karma is the theory that every action, whether seemingly insignificant or not, will boomerang back to the performer with equal force. This means past actions influence the present; present actions influence the future. However, Buddhists interpret karma in a non-linear fashion, leaving open the definition of time and space. They believe things you do in this moment can influence the present, the future, or even your past. In Christianity, the Bible teaches, "Whatsoever a man soweth, that shall he also reap." (Galatians 6:7). Further, the Bible teaches you exactly how to put this principle into practice to attain your goals: "Ask and it will be given to you; seek and you will find; knock and the door will be opened to you." (Matthew 7:7). We have all but to open ourselves to the possibilities; the world of potential is our oyster.

Crown Jewel: The law of cause and effect is a universal law that operates whether you believe in it or not. You are ALWAYS at cause.

Wherever you choose to place your attention, you are at cause. Cause and effect is the premise of using the power of focus. When I discussed the idea that what you focus on gets bigger, you learned that where your attention goes, your energy flows. Whatever you focus your attention on dominates. The power of your focus attracts energy, making it grow. You can sit back and let your unconscious mind lead your attention, or you can consciously control where you lead your mind. If you find you have negative patterns of attention, you will want to use your conscious mind to redirect your attention over and over again until you make it a habit to focus on the positives; however, if you have already trained your unconscious mind to go in the direction you prefer, you can allow it to guide you.

You may often experience the "effect" of your attention immediately; at other times you will not discover the "effects" of your attention for years. The unconscious can have its attention on things we are unaware of, so they may become bigger before we even notice that the unconscious was "causing" them. You may have been putting on weight and not even notice until one day when your pants don't fit. Then you decide you must lose a few pounds, so you review your diet and exercise routine only to realize that you have slacked off on your eating habits and exercise regimen without even realizing it, thus causing the weight gain. Your unconscious, in seeking immediate pleasure, released its habits of clean eating and exercise. Once you regain conscious eating and exercise habits, you can shape up. You can make your revised eating and exercise routines your new habits by practicing them over and over until they are once again ingrained in the unconscious.

You are always at cause in your life, even if it doesn't feel or look like it. Review everything that affects your energy; choose to consciously "cause" it to be what you want. Look at those people you surround yourself with. Look at the profession you've chosen. Look at the spaces you live and work in. You are always, always at the cause. It may be that your choice to study a subject in school led you to your current employment. It may be that your choice to live in close proximity to your family led you to your current home. It may be that your choice to follow your culture led you to your religious beliefs. Now knowing that you are always at cause, choose your cause, therefore choosing your effect. Don't let your unconscious habits steer you down a path you don't want. Choose how you live your life, who you spend your time with, and the energy you circulate in your home and office.

Crown Jewel: You are always at cause. Choose your "cause," therefore choosing your effect. Choose your energy by choosing who you hang around, choose what you feed your mind, and choose what surrounds you.

Tie it all Together with a Big Red Bow

We are all continuous works in process, always growing and learning in every experience. Our greatest lessons come when things aren't perfect. We are all perfect, yet none of us will ever be perfect. My purpose is served if I take all the lessons and make my life, and the lives of those around me, better than they would have been had I not experienced the growth. You are constantly transforming to become an even more exceptional woman, learning the next lesson on your personal path. In reading this book, you are taking a shortcut—you are learning from my lessons.

What a gift I received in being able to give of myself. I am filled with gratitude to offer all my knowledge and services to all the amazing women I am assisting on their paths, and to you. I am thrilled that all the reading, studying, training, practicing, immersion, and repetition that have changed my life, to make it beyond what I could have wished for, is now of service to others. I am so blessed to have received this wisdom for myself and to have been afforded the opportunity to share it in such a positive, fun way—self-development and dating: my favorite two things to do. This book is really all about how to release that exceptional woman within you burning with desire—desire to light the world on fire with your spirit and energy. I see who you really are, and I appreciate your depth, your beauty, and your willingness to learn.

Give yourself the biggest gift ever: self-love, self-esteem, self-worth, and self-respect. Take all these skills and show up in the world as the incredible, exceptional woman you are. This game called life is so exciting; have fun with it, play out fully. Enjoy every moment. Live in the present; it's such a gift. You will have everything you desire in yourself and from the world when you fully expose the exceptional woman you already are—the exceptional woman who will be nothing less than irresistible to your exceptional man. You are a brilliant diamond, allow your radiance to be seen. Let your new mantra be, "This little light of mine, I'm gonna let it shine."

Text Acronym Dictionary

2	To
24/7	24 hours a day, 7 days a week
411	Information
4GT	Forgot/Forget

A

ABT	About
AFAIK	As far as I know
AKA	Also known as
ASAP	As soon as possible

B

B/C	Because
B/W	Between
B4	Before
BCC	Blind carbon copy
BF	Boyfriend
BFF	Best friends forever
BRB	Be right back
BTW	By the way

C

CC	Carbon copy
CTN	Can't talk now
C YA	See ya

CYA	Cover your a**

D

DM	Direct message
DEF	Definitely
DIY	Do it yourself
DOB	Date of Birth

E

ETA	Estimated time of arrival
EZ	Easy

F

F	Female
F2F	Face-to-Face
FAQ	Frequently asked questions
FB	Facebook
FUBAR	F*** up beyond all recognition
FYE	For your entertainment
FYI	For your information

G

G2G	Good to go
GB	Goodbye
GF	Girlfriend
GR8	Great
GTG	Got-to-go

H

H8	Hate
hw	Homework

I

IDK	I don't know
IG	Instagram
IDT	I don't think
IKR	I know right
ILU	I love you
ILY	I love you
IM	Instant Message
IMO	In my opinion
IRL	In real life

J

JIC	Just in case
JK	Just kidding

K

K	OK
KWIM?	Know what I mean?

L

L8	Late
L8R	Later
LMAO	Laughing my a** off
LMK	Let me know
LOL	Laugh out loud

M	Male
MMB	Message me back
MSG	Message
MYOB	Mind your own business

N	
N/A	Not Available
NBD	No big deal
NC	No comment
NE1	Anyone
NM	Not much
NP	No problem
NSFW	Not safe for work
NTK	Need/Nice to know
NVM	Never mind

O	
OBO	Or best offer
OFC	Of course
OMG	Oh my gosh/God
OMW	On my way
OTOH	On the other hand

P

PDA	Public display of affection
PHAT	Pretty hot and tempting
PLMK	Please let me know
PLS	Please
PM	Private message
ppl	People

Q

QT	Cutie

R

R	Are
RE	Regarding
ROFL	Rolling on the floor laughing
RSVP	Répondez s'il vous plait /tell me if you're coming please
RTM	Read the manual
RUOK	Are you okay

S

SO	Significant other
SOL	S*** out of luck
SOS	Someone over shoulder
SRY	Sorry
STFU	Shut the f*** up
SUP	What's up

T

TBA	To be announced
TBC	To be continued
TBD	To be determined
TBH	To be honest
TC	Take care
TGIF	Thank God it's Friday
THX	Thanks
TLC	Tender love and care
TMI	Too much information
TTFN	Ta-ta for now
TTYL	Talk to you later
TXT	Text
TY/TU	Thank you

U

U	You
U2	You too
UR	Your
UW	You're welcome

V

VM	Voicemail
VR	Virtual reality

W

W/	With
W/E	Whatever
W/O	Without
W8	Wait
WB	Write back/Welcome Back
WFM	Works for me
WRT	With regard/respect to
WTF	What the F***
WU?	What's up?

X

XOXO	Hugs and kisses
XR	Extended Reality

Y

Y	Why
YGM	You've got mail
YOLO	You only live once
YW	You're welcome

Z

ZZZ	Sleep

Endnotes

[1] Hamlet, ed. Jonathan Bate et al. (New York: Modern Library, 2008) 2.2.254-255.

[2] Marianne Williamson, A Return To Love: Reflections on the Principles of A Course in Miracles, New York: Harper Collins, 1992, 190-191.

[3] Foundation for Inner Peace, A Course in Miracles, Tiburon: The Foundation, 1975.

**PIERUCCI
PUBLISHING**

We're Publishing!

Are you a mindful author, entrepreneur, coach, or healer looking to contribute your wisdom to the new world awakening?

Pierucci Publishing is committed to publishing just 121 Conscious Authors in 2021.

Are you one of them?

Please find us at www.PierucciPublishing.com to apply.

Made in the USA
Coppell, TX
08 May 2022